Duct Tape Crafts

3rd Edition

67 Ultimate Duct Tape Crafts – For Purses, Wallets & Much More!

by Kitty Moore

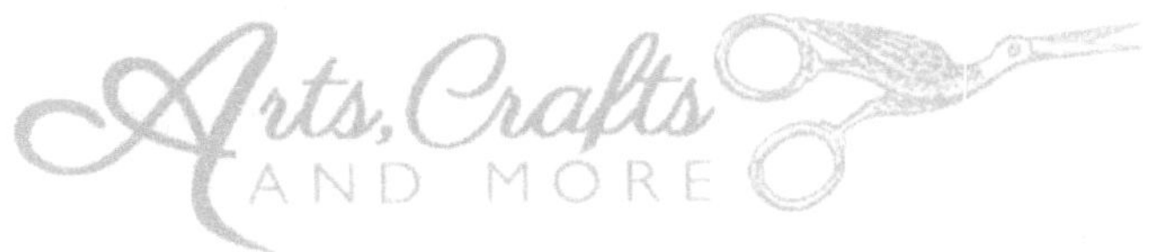

Table of Contents

Introduction

When we were kids, I will never forget how all that was needed to make my brother happy was a few sticks and a couple of rolls of duct tape. He used these to make endless varieties of toys, cars, and guns for himself, and it was amazing to see what he used to come up with.

Duct tape has come a long way since then. Back then, you only really got a few plain colors. Now duct tape comes in a range of colors and patterns. You can even find duct tape with a fabric finish!

With all these great patterns and colors available, there is no reason to not let your imagination run free with duct tape.

It is relatively inexpensive, and projects can be completed in a matter of hours without a lot of mess.

This is the ideal craft to keep the kids happy on a rainy day or even to keep mom happy and relaxed.

In this book, I will share my favorite duct tape projects and teach you some basic tricks for making duct tape crafts.

Once you understand the basics, you are free to let your own imagination take over. Just imagine what wonderful projects you can come up with on your own.

Happy crafting!

1. Duct Tape Fabric

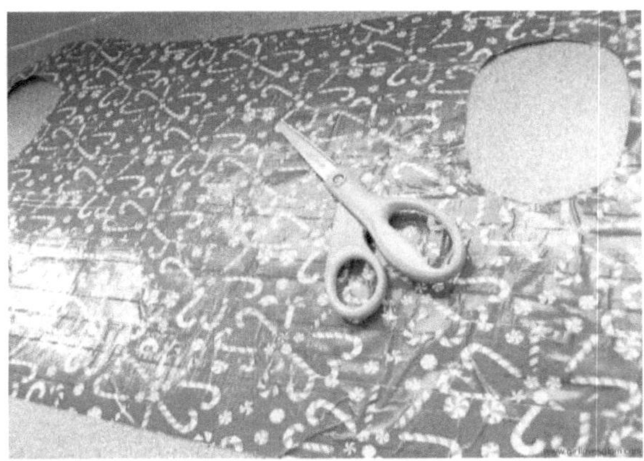

Materials

- Duct tape
- Scissors or craft knife
- Ruler

Directions

1. This is a basic skill you need to learn if you want to really get creative with your duct tape crafts. Making a basic fabric will make it possible for you to make bags, wallets, etc. from duct tape – items that require a bit more durability. Figure out how big a piece of "fabric" you want and cut your strips of duct tape a little longer than that.

2. Lay the first strip on the table, adhesive side facing up. Place the second strip in the same way, making sure that there is a little overlap between the pieces – the more the overlap, the tighter the weave of the "fabric" will be and the stronger the tape will be.

3. Now cut strips that are slightly longer than the width of your fabric and place them, in the same manner as above, one

slightly overlapping the other, adhesive side facing up, so that you have two pieces of "fabric".

4. Place the two pieces, adhesive side together, one on top of the other so that they match. Trim any excess material.

5. You now have a sheet of "fabric" that you can use for other projects. If you want a stronger "fabric", you can add more layers of duct tape, keeping in mind that the more layers there are, the less flexible the "fabric" becomes.

2. Duct Tape Wallet

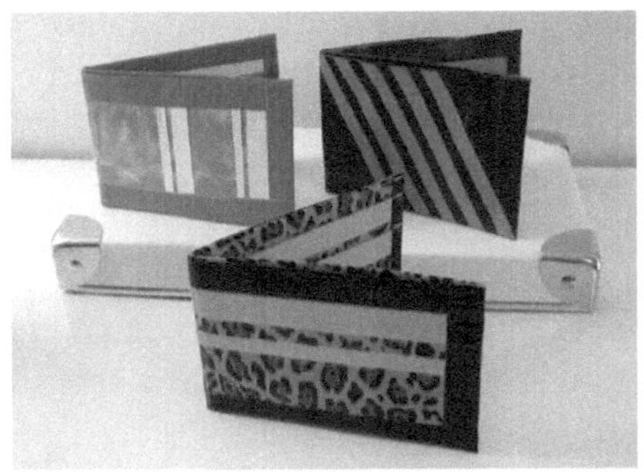

Materials

- Ruler
- Duct tape
- Pencil
- Scissors or utility knife

Directions

1. Cut out four pieces of duct tape, about 10 inches long each. Lay down the first strip of tape, with the non-adhesive side facing your work surface.

2. Lay the second strip down in the same manner, allowing the pieces to overlap by about ¼ inch. Do the same with the remaining strips. Your end piece of "fabric" should measure around about 10 inches by 7 inches. Repeat the procedure and make another sheet. Match up the two sheets and stick together using the adhesive areas left over.

3. Cut another strip of duct tape, 10 inches long. Taking your scissors, make a cut at the middle of the strip's one end. Cut no more than an inch in length, and then rip the piece of tape in half. These strips will be used to seal the 10-inch edges of the sheet.

4. Now measure out 9 inches of your "fabric," and cut the sheet so that it measures 9 inches across. Fold your "fabric" in two equal halves, lengthwise. Following the same steps, make two even strips that are 4 inches long and 1-inch wide. Use these strips to tape up the outside edges of your strip and trim the edges to neaten them.

5. Now you have the basic body done, you can now make the wallet pocket. You need two pieces of tape, 5 inches long and 2 inches wide. With the adhesive sides facing, stick these two pieces together.

6. Cut another 5-inch strip and tear in half. Use this to seal the top edge of the pocket. Use the remaining piece of tape to stick the pocket into the wallet by sticking down the unsealed edge.

7. Trim down the sides so that the pocket is exactly the right size. Cut another strip of duct tape, long enough to close off the shorter sides of the wallet. Tear this strip in half and use to finish off your wallet.

3. Duct Tape Men's Tie

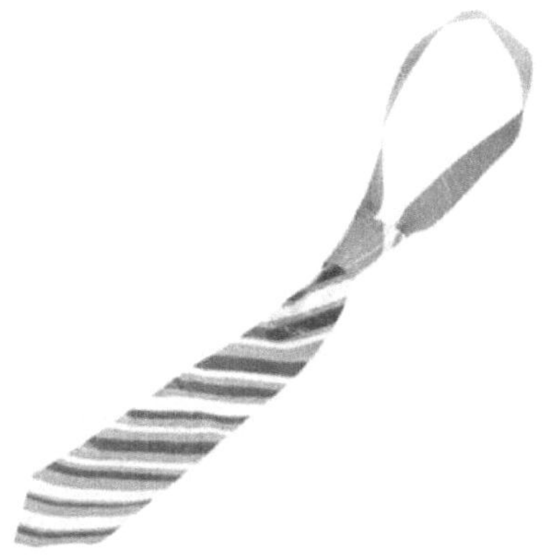

Materials

- Tie to use as a template
- Scissors
- Duct tape
- A permanent marker

Directions

1. Lay the tie out flat on the table. Measure the tie from the thinnest end to where it starts to taper and become wider.

2. Cut two pieces of duct tape this length and place adhesive sides together so that you end up with a piece of "fabric" that is not sticky on either side.

3. Check that the end of your template tie fits onto the tape, and carefully draw around the thin end using your marker. Cut the "fabric" along this outline so that your duct tape matches your template.

4. Seal off all the edges with more duct tape so that the cut edges do not show. This may mean using a lot of smaller

pieces. Now move on to the rest of your tie. Cut three lengths of duct tape to the same length of what is left of your tie.

5. Lay these three pieces out, side-by-side, with the adhesive side facing up.

6. Adhere the first piece to the second, allowing for a slight overlap so that they are adhered well. Repeat with the third piece.

7. Cut several short strips of tape and place them over the three pieces you cut so that they are at a ninety-degree angle. Cover the whole area so that there are no gaps remaining.

8. Repeat steps, this time using the wider side of the tie as a template. Now you have two tie pieces; join them together with duct tape and reinforce the joint.

4. Duct Tape Tote Bag

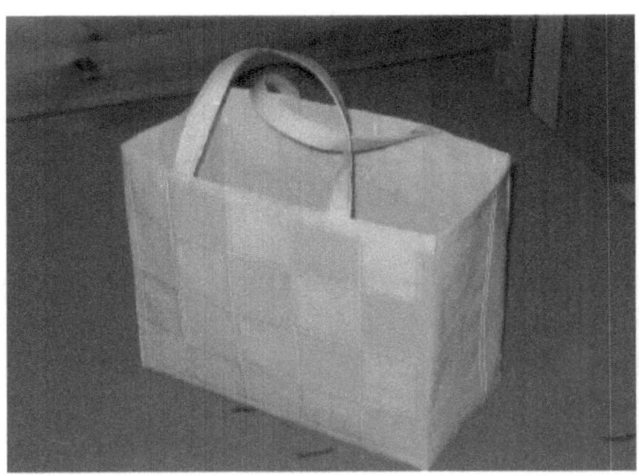

Materials

- Duct tape
- Scissors or a craft knife
- Plain paper
- Ruler

Directions

1. Start by making a template for the bottom by cutting a piece of paper that measures 5.5 inches by 3 inches. Cover the back of this template with duct tape, allowing a bit of overlap between pieces so that they adhere to one another, and trim off any excess.

2. Turn the paper over and repeat the process, this time making sure that the duct tape is at least ¼ inch larger than the template at the longest edges.

3. Set aside and make the sides. Cut strips of duct tape 7 inches long and lay them side-by-side. Again, adhere each strip to the one before it by overlapping a little and make this piece of "fabric" 5.5 inches wide. Make two such pieces of fabric.

4. Stick the two sides of the fabric to your bottom piece, using the adhesive strips you had left in place before. Turn the fabric over and reinforce these seams.

5. You should now have a long piece of fabric measuring around 19.5 inches from end to end. Find the middle point of the bottom of the bag and fold it in half.

6. You now have the basic shape of your tote. Cut two long strips of duct tape and use them to fix the sides of your tote into place. Reinforce the joint with more tape. Trim so that the top edges are straight, if necessary.

7. Now all you need to do is to make the handles. Cut two strips of tape 7 inches long and stick to each other, adhesive sides facing so that there are no sticky edges facing out. Stick this strip into the inside of your bag and adhere with duct tape to reinforce it. Repeat steps for the second handle.

5. Duct Tape Crystal Bracelet

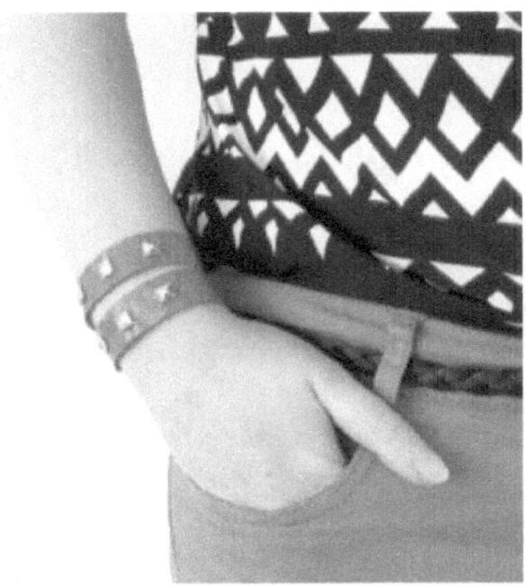

Materials

- Crystal sheet (in a color of your choice)
- Velcro sticky back fastener in a matching color
- Duct tape, (same color as the crystal)
- Vintage brooch

Directions

1. Take a measurement of your wrist and add ¾-inch as a seam allowance. The crystal sheet should be cut to match this length and should be the width of your duct tape.

2. Set the crystal sheet down and remove the two rows of crystals on each edge so you have a place to put the duct tape.

3. Using duct tape, stick the Velcro sticky back fastener to the crystal sheet on one side. On the opposite side of the crystal sheet, repeat this process using the loop side of the fastener. Trim off any excess. Center your brooch at the middle of the crystal sheet, and attach it.

I have included a bonus just for you…

FOR A LIMITED TIME ONLY – Get my best-selling book "DIY Crafts: The 100 Most Popular Crafts & Projects That Make Your Life Easier" absolutely FREE!

Readers who have downloaded the bonus book as well have seen the greatest changes in their crafting abilities and have expanded their repertoire of crafts – so it is *highly recommended* to get this bonus book today!

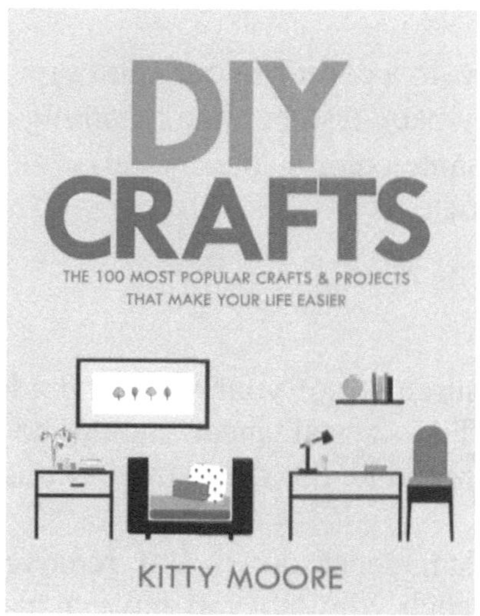

Get your free copy at:

ArtsCraftsAndMore.com/Bonus

6. Phone Case

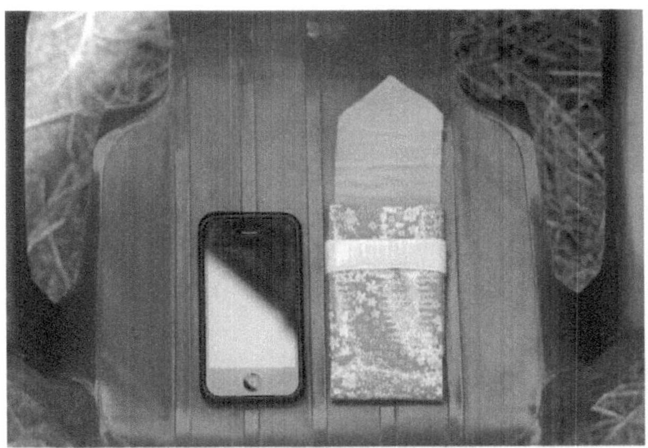

Materials

- Scissors of craft knife
- Duct tape in contrasting colors
- Plain phone case

Directions

1. Cut out shapes from the duct tape. They can be whatever you want.

2. Stick the shapes onto your phone case.

7. Duct Tape Coasters

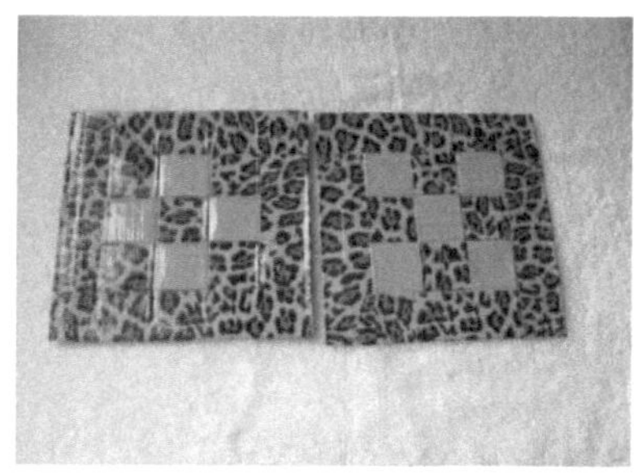

Materials

- Duct tape in two coordinating colors
- Scissors or a craft knife
- Paper

Directions

1. Cut a 4" x 4" square from your paper for each coaster that you want to make. Cover the bottom of the square with a layer of duct tape by adhering it strip by strip, so that each strip slightly overlaps the previous one.

2. Turn the paper over and repeat on the front. Once the paper is covered, it is time to get the design right. Place your coordinating color of duct tape in two strips across the center of coaster.

3. Cut strips of the first color to go over this, but this time, split the strips into equal halves of 1-inch width each. Weave these strips in so that you have a pleasing pattern.

8. Duct Tape Hat

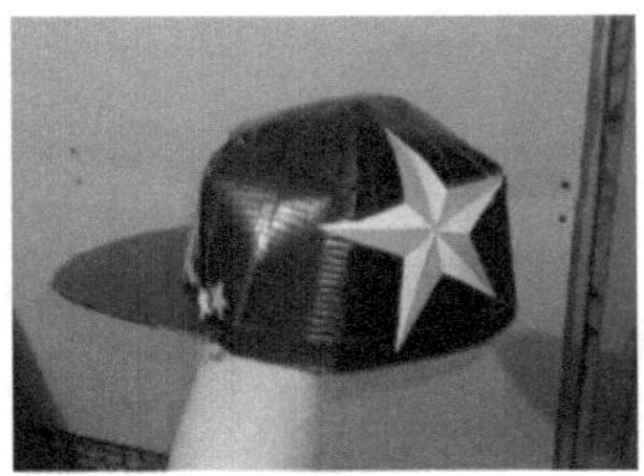

Materials

- Duct tape
- Hat to use as a mold
- Tin foil
- Scissors or craft knife

Directions

1. Cover the hat you are using as a mold in a few layers of tin foil so that you have an accurate base for your new hat.

2. Cut strips of tape, about 2.5 – 3 inches long, and cover the tin foil so that you can no longer see it. A second layer will reinforce the hat. Turn the mold over and remove the hat you originally used to shape it.

3. Cover the inside of the mold with duct tape. You can either use the same color as you did on the outside or a contrasting color for a different look. Trim off the excess around the brim and cover with a strip of tape.

9. Duct Tape Bangles

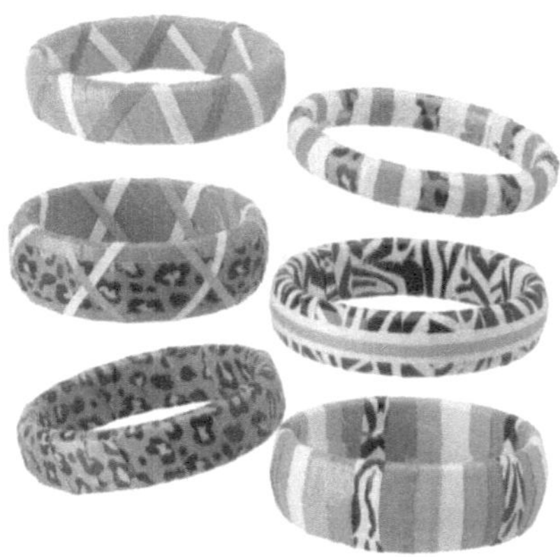

Materials

- Duct tape
- Shower curtain rings or an old plastic or wooden bracelet
- Scissors

Directions

1. This is a really simple project. Wrap your bracelet carefully using one long strand of duct tape. Each edge should overlap slightly.

2. The key here is to get a really smooth, even finish.

10. 3D Flowers with Duct Tape

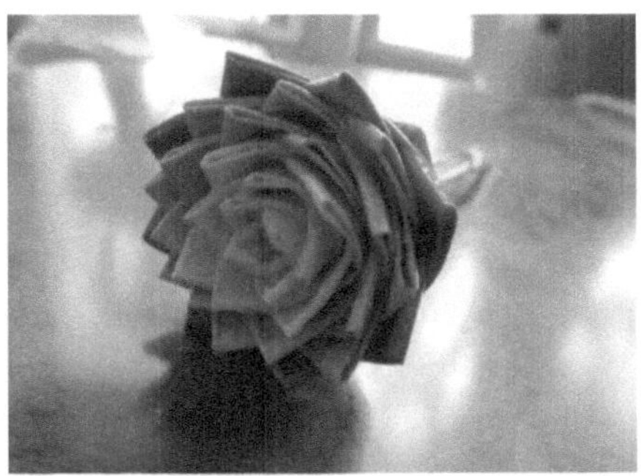

Materials

- Duct tape (one green roll and the other a color of your choice)
- 3D flower die
- Thin card
- Scissors
- Hot glue gun and glue
- Toothpicks (optional)

Directions

1. Cover the card in an even layer of duct tape – none of the card should show through. A slight overlap of each layer gives the best results.

2. Use your die to cut out the flower shape and to mold it into the basic shape. Glue securely using the hot glue gun, and set it aside to dry.

3. You can use the flowers as is for paper crafts or jewelry, or you make a stem for them by covering the entire toothpick (except for one pointed end) with green duct tape. Push the pointed edge into the rose, and fix in place with glue.

11. Duct Tape Covered Notebook

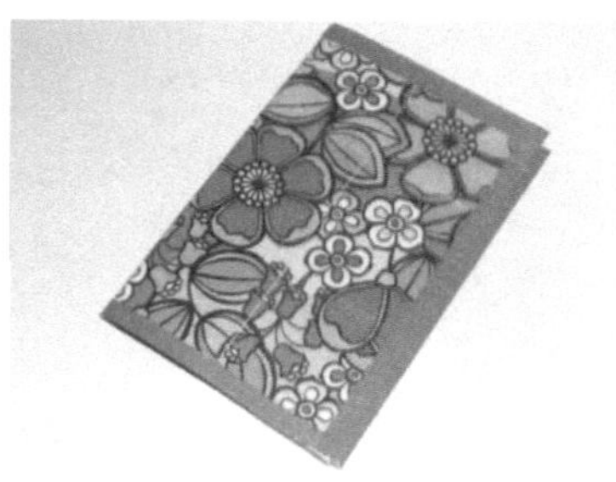

Materials

- Duct tape
- Notebook
- Scissors

Directions

1. Open your notebook to the center pages and place it face down on your work surface. Measure the length of the notebook. Cut strips of duct tape to match and lay each strip lengthwise, with the last strip slightly overlapping the strip before it.

2. Continue in this manner until the entire book is covered. If you choose, you can overlap this layer with a contrasting layer of tape.

3. If you decide to have a contrasting color, close the book first, and then lay strips widthwise. If you do not use enough duct tape, you may find that the book becomes difficult to close. This will make your cover water-resistance and durable.

12. Duct Tape Shoe Revamp

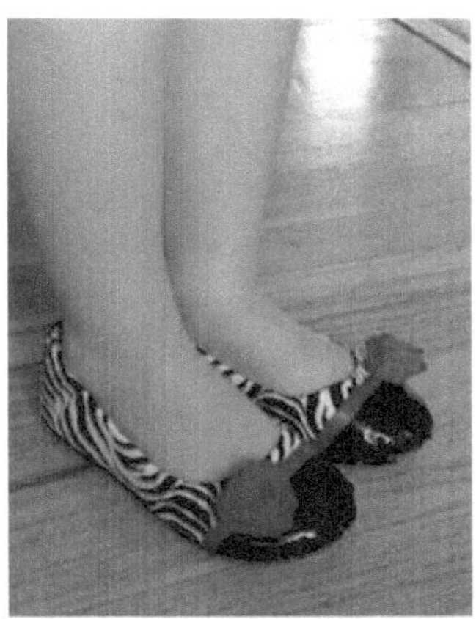

Materials

- Old pair of shoes/boots
- Duct tape with a funky pattern
- Scissors
- Craft knife

Directions

1. This is ideal for a pair of shoes that is starting to look scuffed or old. Wipe down the outside of the shoes using a damp cloth and warm soapy water so that there is no debris, and set them aside to dry.

2. Start by covering the back of the shoe. If the heel still looks good leave it uncovered. Just be sure that the color coordinates with your duct tape.

3. The back of the shoe is fairly easy to cover. Use a shorter piece of duct tape and make sure that it is flat against the shoe. Overlap each piece slightly, and leave a little bit of excess where the shoe meets the sole.

4. Working on the toe of the shoe is more difficult because of the curve. Cutting slits into the duct tape will allow you to follow the curve more closely. Again, get it to lie as flat as possible. Cover the entire shoe.

5. Where you have left the excess, tuck it into the sole as far as you can so that you cannot see the original finish of the shoe. Carefully trim the excess with your craft knife so that you don't cut the shoe.

13. Duct Tape Drum

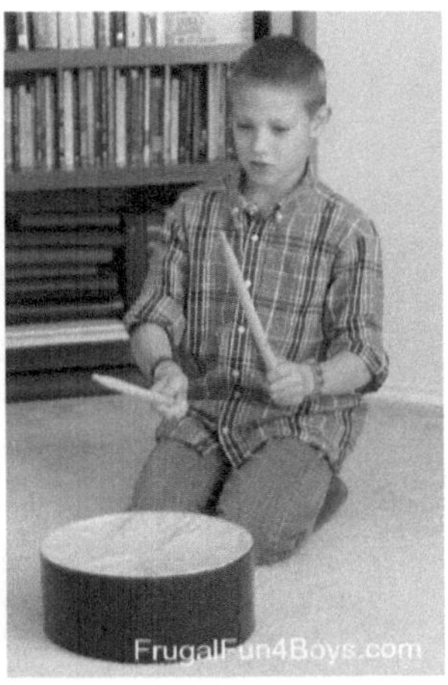

Materials

- Old large can (a coffee can is ideal although you can use a smaller can if necessary)
- Duct tape
- Scissors

Directions

1. Close off any sharp edges on the tin with duct tape. Stretch duct tape over the open mouth of the tin and about two inches down the side of each side of the tin, each strip of tape should overlap the previous strip a little so that there are no gaps. This will form your drum skin.

2. Carefully wrap the sides of the tin with duct tape. This helps to secure the layers used for the drum skin.

14. DIY Office Filing System

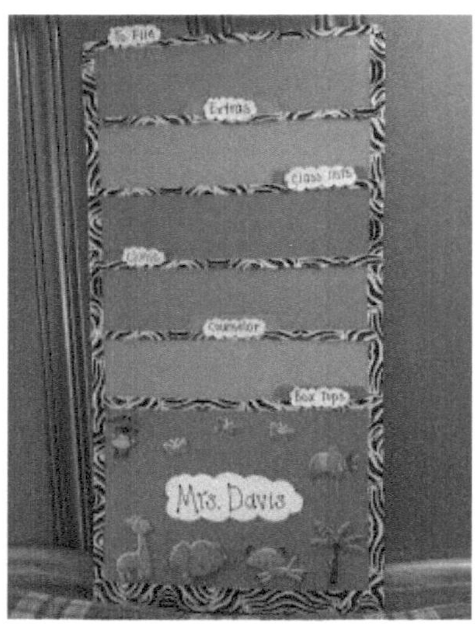

Materials

- 3 Cereal boxes (all the same size)
- Duct tape
- Scissors
- Ruler
- Glue

Directions

1. Cut the tops off of each of the cereal boxes. Glue each box on top of the other so that you have a stack of boxes. If you want to, seal the cut edges of the box with some duct tape.

2. Wrap duct tape around the outer edges of the stack to make sure that it is secure and more durable.

15. Duct Tape Vase

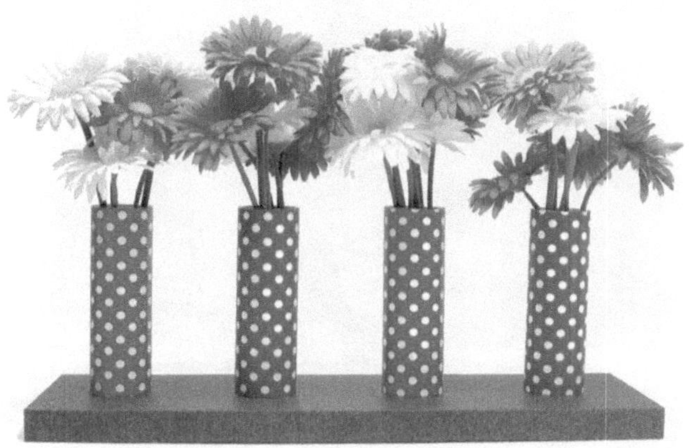

Materials

- An empty plastic or glass container
- Duct tape
- Scissors

Directions

1. If needed, cut the container down to a suitable size. If it is pretty much the right size already, cut off the lip. (If you are using glass, skip this step).

2. Cover the entire outside of the container with duct tape, overlapping each strip so that nothing of the original container shows through. If you are battling to get the duct tape to lie flat, slit it slightly so that it can fit better over the curves. Finish off by covering the lip of the container.

16. Easy Duct Tape Cuffs

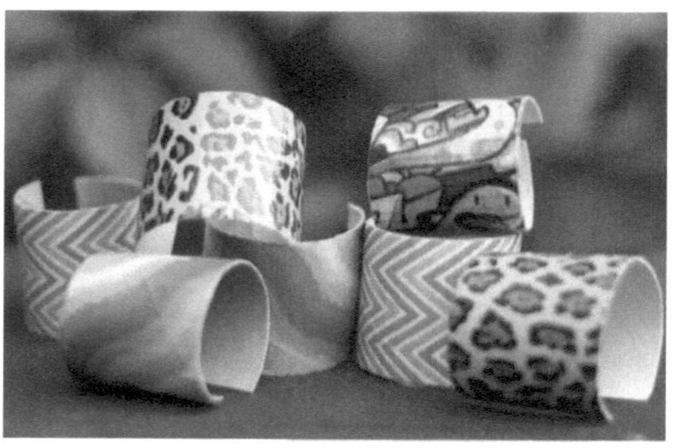

Materials

- Toilet paper tubes
- Duct Tape
- Scissors

Directions

1. Cut the toilet paper tubes to the length that you want the cuffs to be and slit them down the middle so that they can easily stretch to fit on someone's arm.

2. Cover the outside of the tube with duct tape, making sure that each layer overlaps the previous one and that you also cover the open edges that you slit earlier.

3. Cover with a second layer of duct tape for additional strength. You may also cover the edges of the tube with 1-inch wide strips of duct tape in a contrasting color to create a more interesting finish.

17. Clever Duct Tape Chain

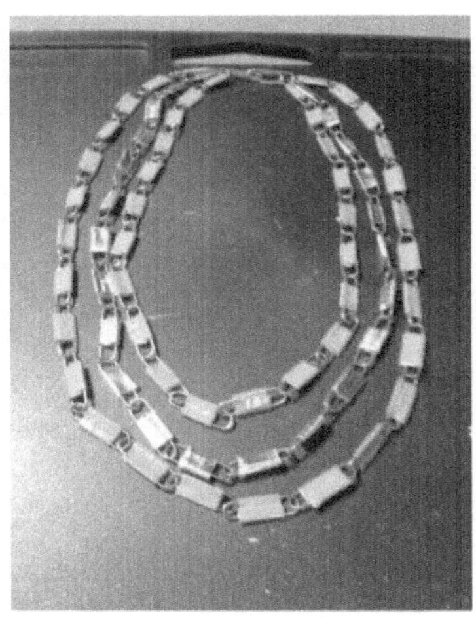

Materials

- Duct tape (choose a couple of different colors or patterns)
- Paper clips
- Scissors

Directions

1. This craft takes a little longer, but it allows you to make interesting chains and accessories in the latest fashion colors for pennies! And when the trend is over, you feel no guilt when you stop wearing them.

2. Start off by interlacing the paper clips until you have a chain the length that you desire. Be sure that it is long enough to fit over your head.

3. Cut small strips of duct tape and cover your paper clips. Make sure that all the join lines are to the same side so that your necklace has a front and a backside.

18. Laptop Bag

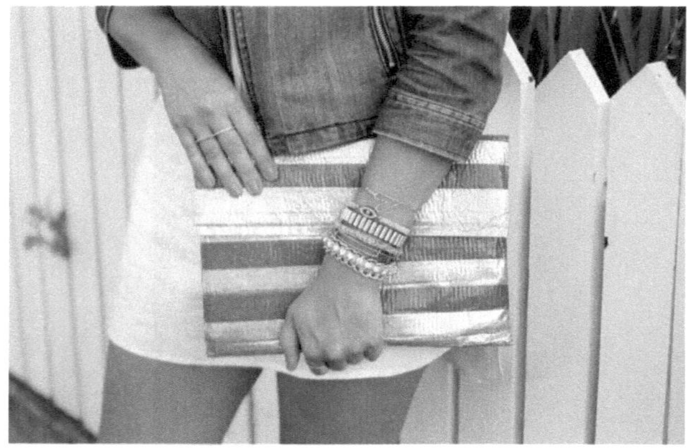

Materials

- Old or new laptop bag
- Duct tape in coordinating colors
- Scissors
- Ruler
- Paper
- Pencil
- Dressmaker's pencil (optional)

Directions

1. Measure out the dimensions of the laptop bag, and find a piece of paper about the same size. Plan your design using the paper and pencil or print out a suitable design from the internet. Geometric shapes with straight lines will work better here. If you are unsure whether the design will look good when finished, make it up on the paper first.

2. If you like, you can transfer the design to the laptop case using a white dressmaker's pencil. Alternatively, measure out the design and build it up directly onto the case that way.

3. Create fabric with the duct tape in the colors you would like for your pattern. Use the fabric to create the design either over the paper or the laptop case. Cut thin strips of duct tape to secure the design down around the edges. You can either use the same color as the main design or a contrasting color.

19. Duct Tape Hair Bows

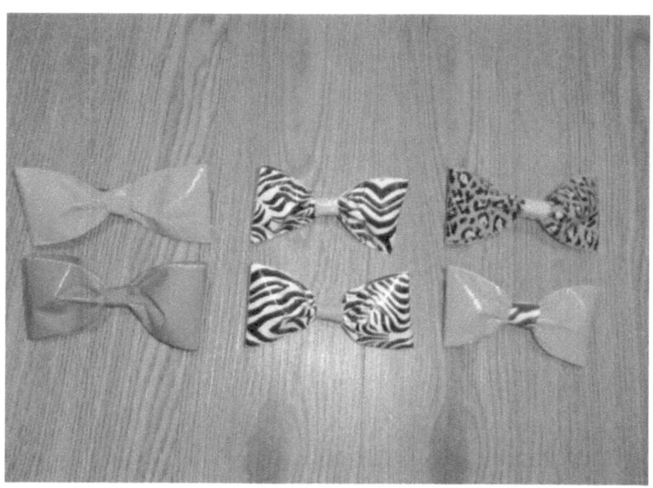

Materials

- Duct tape in two contrasting colors
- Scissors
- Elastic head band

Directions

1. Depending on the size you want the bow to be, you may need to join two or three pieces of duct tape together. Cut the tape to the width that you are looking for, and then build up the length of your "fabric."

2. Trim your fabric to the right size, and make three equal folds in the center so that you can pinch the bow into shape.

3. Once you have the shape you are looking for, using your contrasting duct tape, fasten the bow around the center. Place the elastic hair band flat against the back of your bow, and secure it using another two pieces of the contrasting duct tape.

20. Duct Tape Cushions for A Dollhouse

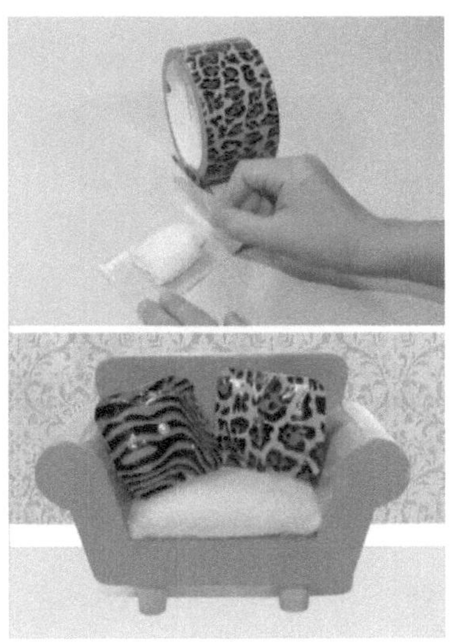

Materials

- Duct tape
- Scissors
- Cotton wool

Directions

1. Making cool accessories for a little girl's dollhouse has never been easier. Start by measuring the chairs in the dollhouse. You want the cushions to fit nicely.

2. Cut your tape to double the length of the desired measurement of the cushions. Place with the adhesive side up onto the table.

3. Place cotton wool in the center, leaving a little bit of the adhesive showing on all sides so that the cushion can be securely closed. Fold the tape in half and make sure that all the edges are secure and you have a little pillow.

21. Duct Tape Beads

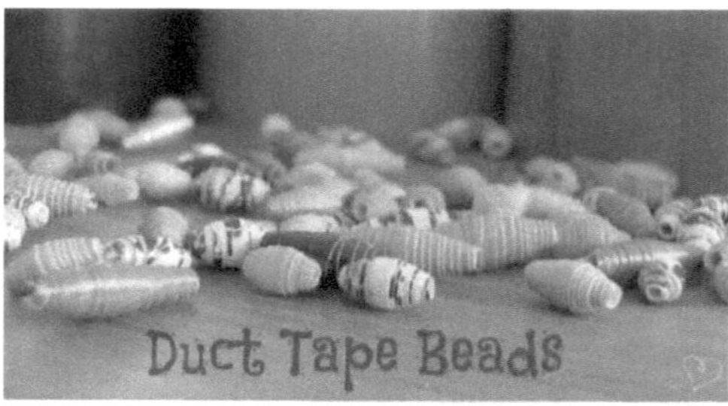

Materials

- Duct tape
- Scissors
- Drinking straws

Directions

1. This one is a lot easier than making beads with strips of magazine paper because of the adhesiveness of the tape. You can also cut longer strips from the duct tape than you can from your magazine pages, and there is no need to varnish the beads afterwards. The beads do tend to be a little bulkier though. The longer the strip, the bulkier the bead. The wider the strip, the wider the bead.

2. Cut your duct tape into long strips and then cut those strips into long triangles. This gives the bead a more tapered shape in the middle. Alternatively, simply tear the strip into two 1-inch pieces that are straight, and use that for a bead that is more tubular.

3. Taking the longer side of the duct tape, attach it to one of the straws and then wind it onto the straw slowly and evenly. At the end, the thickest part of the bead should be in the middle and the bead should be even, so be careful not to go off track. Snip the finished bead off the end of the straw and start with your next one.

22. Duct Tape Belt

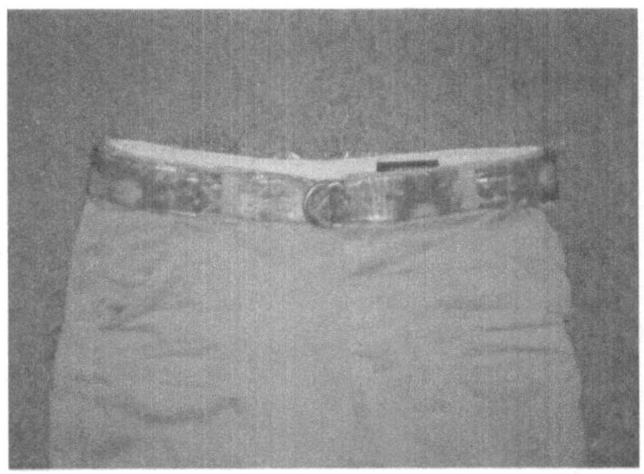

Materials

- Duct tape
- Scissors
- 2 D-rings

Directions

1. Measure around the waist to get the measurement needed for the belt. Add on an extra 5 inches to the length to allow for the D-rings. If you want a wider belt, leave the duct tape as is. If you want a narrower belt, then you just need to fold the duct tape in half.

2. Cut the length of duct tape to the measurements determined in Step 1. If you are using the duct tape as is, cut a second strip, the same length as the first and lay it on top of the first strip, adhesive sides facing, so that the end strip is not sticky at all. Alternatively, fold the strip in half.

3. Slide the D-rings onto the duct tape and fold it over so that they are enclosed in a loop, use no more than two inches of your "belt" for this – secure with another strip of tape. You can now wear the belt! Fasten it with the D-rings.

23. Duct Tape Pencil Holder

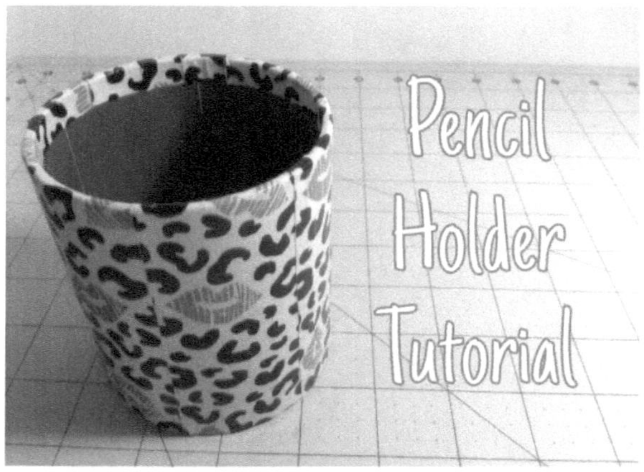

Materials

- A tin can (thoroughly washed and dried)
- Duct tape
- Scissors

Directions

1. Make sure that all sharp edges of the can are removed. Alternatively, cover the inside edge of the mouth of the can with duct tape. Try to use one strand of tape if at all possible for a much neater finish.

2. Starting at the base of the tin, wind the duct tape up around the tin so that each layer overlaps slightly with the previous one. If needed, apply a second layer of tape.

24. Duct Tape Earrings

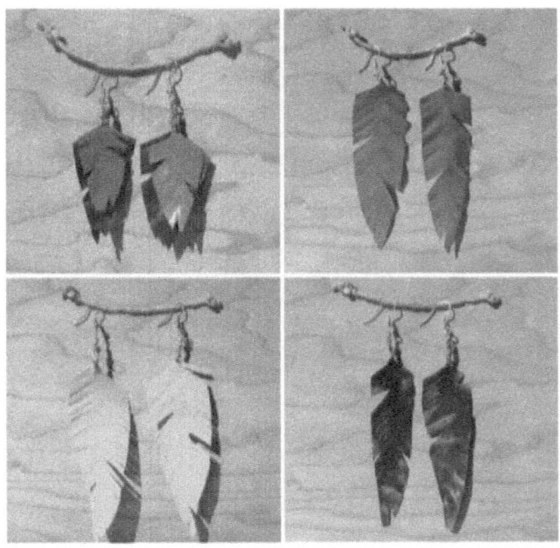

Materials

- Duct tape in the color of your choice
- Scissors
- 2 sets of pliers (needle nose works best)
- Thin wire
- A Pencil
- A set of earring hooks

Directions

1. Cut a length of duct tape about 6 inches long and fold in half, sticky sides facing each other so that no adhesive sides are showing. This will create one feather so repeat as desired.

2. Draw the rough shape of a feather – if you are not too confident, download a template online to help you. Cut out the basic shape.

3. Cut short slits along the length of the "feather" to get the right texture. The slits should be angled up toward the tip of your feather. The more slits, the more feathery it will look.

4. Every few slits or so, cut a little triangle out – make it random so that it looks more natural. Twist the feather a bit so that it looks more realistic.

5. When you are happy with the results, cut a 3-inch piece of wire and wrap around the base of the feather (the stem). Hold the feather in one pair of pliers and us the other to hold the wire.

6. Wrap the "stem" of the feather with the wire and secure it properly, leaving a small bit at the end so that you can make a loop that can be attached to the earring hook. Be sure to pinch in the end of the wire so that there are no harsh edges.

7. Take your earring hook and open the bottom ring. Attach your feather and you're done. Repeat with the other feather.

25. Up-Cycled Hoop Earrings

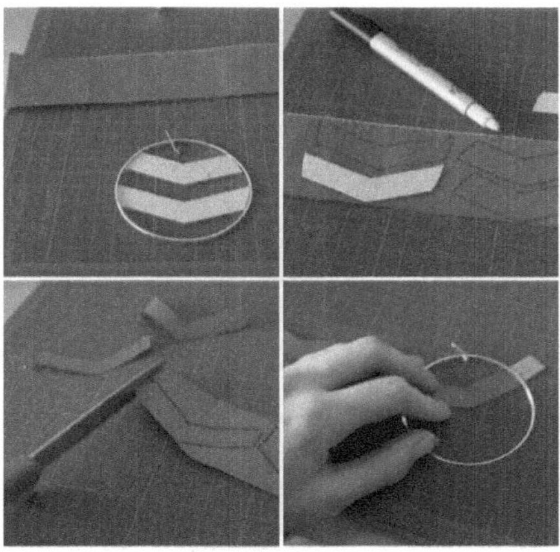

Materials

- An old pair of hoop earrings
- Scissors
- Duct tape in your choice of color
- Glue

Directions

1. Cut a 6-inch strip of duct tape and fold it in half, sticky sides together so that no adhesive is showing. Trace the outside circle of the hoop earring onto the duct tape. Make two circles so they are identical.

2. Sketch whatever design you like, using the circles drawn as a guide to get the size right. For this project, we used chevrons but you can choose whatever design you like.

3. Cut the shapes out carefully and lay them on the outside of the hoops. Cut small bits of duct tape to use to secure the shapes into place. One piece for each side. Tape onto the back of the hoop so that the duct tape is not visible. Trim as necessary.

26. Punk Style Earrings

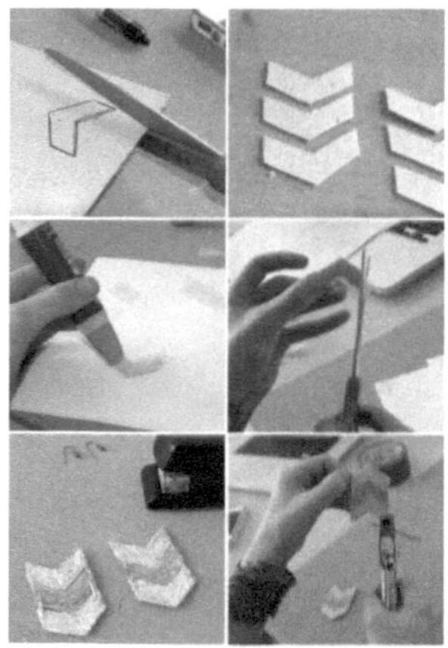

Materials

- Pieces of cardstock
- Duct tape in colors of your choice
- Odds and ends of lace
- A stapler and staples
- A length of chain
- Earring hooks
- Clear adhesive
- Jump rings
- Needle nose pliers
- A set of wire cutters

Directions

1. Either download a chevron design or draw one freehand onto the piece of cardstock. This will be a template for all of your pieces.

2. Cut a 12-inch strip of duct tape and fold it in half so that the adhesive side is facing in. Trace the shape of the chevron onto this "fabric." You will need 6 pieces.

3. Using the cardstock as a template cut 6 pieces from the lace.

4. Glue these in place on the chevron duct tape pieces, and set them aside to dry. Trim the lace as necessary.

5. Each earring will consist of three of these chevrons Lay them next to one another and staple them together.

6. Punch a hole in the bottom edges of each chevron (the point of the chevrons should point down). The holes will be on the upper edges.

7. Cut two bits of chain. The longer these bits are, the lower the earrings will hang.

8. Open the jump rings and attach one end of each piece of chain to the holes you made. Use a third jump ring to join the other ends of the chain, and then attach them to the earring hooks. Repeat to create the other earring.

27. Quick Ring Accessory

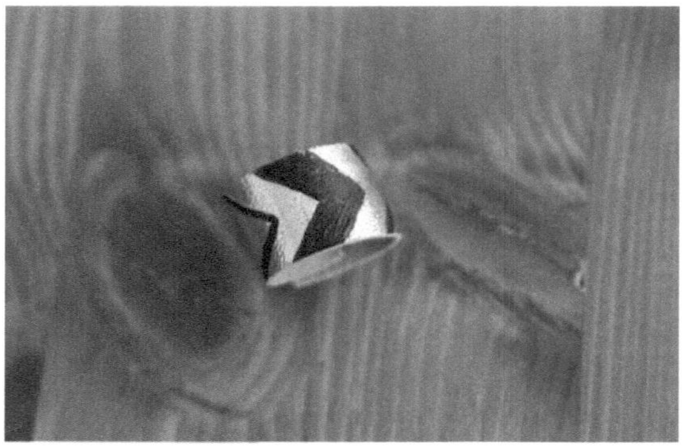

Materials

- Duct tape in the colors of your choice
- Acrylic paint and brush or sharpies
- Adhesive
- A snap button

Directions

1. Cut a 6-inch strip of duct tape and fold in half so that none of the adhesive shows.

2. Cut it down to ¾ inch wide strip. Make it long enough to go over your finger and add enough of an overlap so that there is space for the snap button.

3. Paint the tape as required (simple bold shapes are easiest for a big impact) and set them aside to dry. Glue on the snap button pieces individually.

28. Pretty Heart Pendant

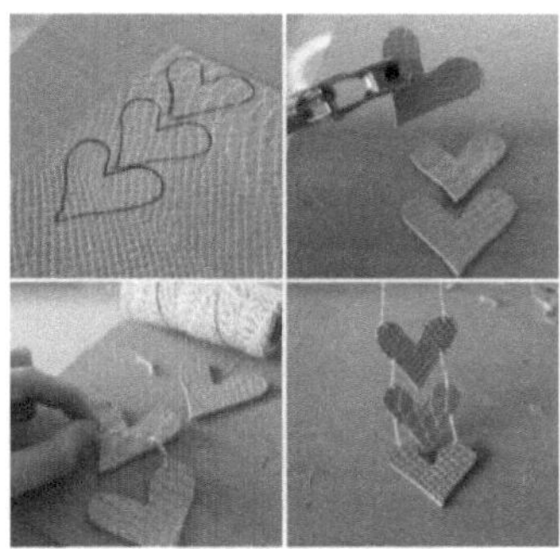

Materials

- Duct tape in the colors of your choice
- A piece of cardstock
- Thin twine
- A hole puncher
- Craft knife

Directions

1. Cut a 10-inch strip of duct tape and fold it in half, adhesive sides facing together so that no adhesive shows. Cut three more strips that are 5 inches in length and lay on top of the first so that they adhere to it.

2. Draw a heart freehand on a piece of cardstock to use as a template. Cut three hearts out of your "fabric." Line them up next to one another (as seen in the picture) and mark out where the holes for the twine would need to go. Punch the holes as required.

3. Take a length of twine that is at least double the length required to make your final necklace. Thread one end of the twine through each hole on the left side and knot securely. Repeat with the other end of the twine on the right side, adjusting the length as desired.

29. Ultra-Cool Duct Tape Cuff

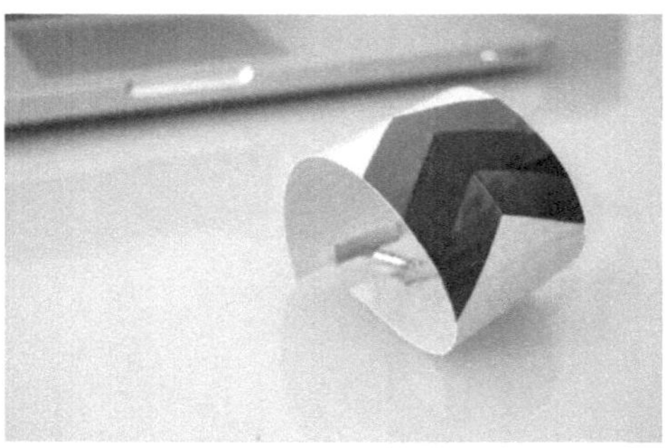

Materials

- Duct tape in 3 bright colors
- A lobster clasp
- 2 fastener clips
- Strong adhesive
- Needle nose pliers

Directions

1. Cut a piece of tape in your main color that is 12 inches long and fold in half, ensuring that no adhesive shows. Trim to fit your wrist, taking into account the length of the lobster clasp. You don't want it to be too loose.

2. Lay your second color over the middle of the first – creating the design as desired. Your third color tape is now ready to be laid. This design should be the smallest of all. Glue the fastener clips onto either end of the strip of duct tape. Attach the lobster clasp, and you are done.

30. Braided Ring

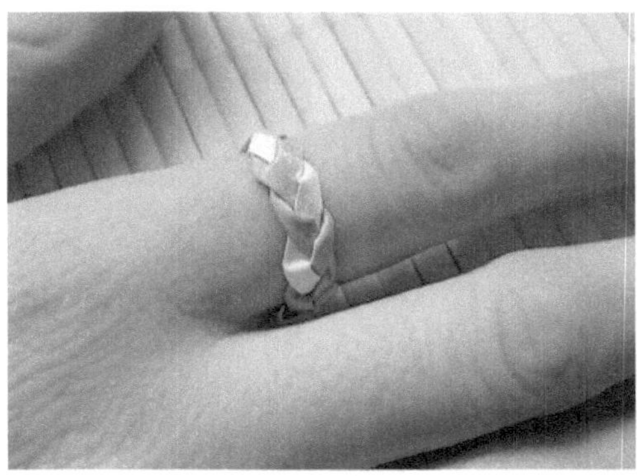

Materials

- Duct tape in two or three contrasting colors
- Sharp scissors
- A plastic board

Directions

1. You will not easily be able to adjust the end length of the ring, so make sure to measure properly first. The tape should fit around your finger with an extra ¾ inch.

2. Tear or cut this strip into three equal parts. Set aside one strip for use. The others can be used in a different project. You will do the same for each of the colors of tape so that you end up with 3 strips.

3. Fold the strip in half lengthwise, sticky side outside to find the exact center. Make a cut about halfway from the end of the strip to this mid-point. Repeat on the opposite end, making sure that the cut is diagonally opposite to the first. Repeat for each of the strips.

4. Unfold each strip and refold lengthwise, this time with the adhesive sides facing each other. The adhesive sides will now

be completely covered, except for the half-inch that you cut out before. These will be facing in different directions. Cut each of these strips into thirds again, lengthwise. If you check the duct tape, you should be able to see that there are threads running along its length. Cut using these as a guide.

5. Now you can start braiding. Place your first strip onto your plastic board, adhering it to the surface using one of the sticky bits faced down. Stick the second strip on top of the same end, at around about a 30-degree angle to the first.

6. Place the last strip in the same way, but position it halfway between the first and third strips. Start braiding from the right and continue until the whole strip is braided. Work slowly and methodically to ensure that the braid remains smooth. When you get to the end, place each of the sticky bits together so that the braid is secure.

7. Wrap on your finger to check the size and then adhere the remaining sticky bits so that the ring is complete. Cut a small strip of duct tape (just long enough to cover the joint). Wrap this strip around the joint.

31. Duct Tape Mask

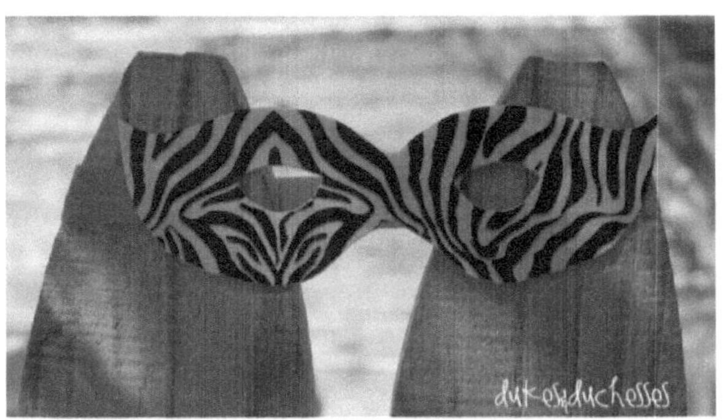

Materials

- Patterned duct tape of your choice
- Double-sided elastic in a coordinating color
- A candle and matches
- A mask template

Directions

1. Cut a piece of duct tape about 8 inches wide, and lay it on a flat surface sticky side up. Cut a second piece the same length and lay it down on the first, sticky side up, so that there is an overlap of about a quarter inch. Repeat until your "fabric is big enough to fit your mask template.

2. Once the size is right, cut an equal number of strips and repeat the process, this time with the sticky side facing down. No adhesive should be showing.

3. Using your template, or a freehand drawing, trace your mask shape onto the "fabric" and cut it out. Cut enough elastic so that the mask will fit around the head comfortably and seal the ends using the candle and matches. Secure the elastic to the back of your mask using a strip of duct tape.

32. Duct Tape Watch Band

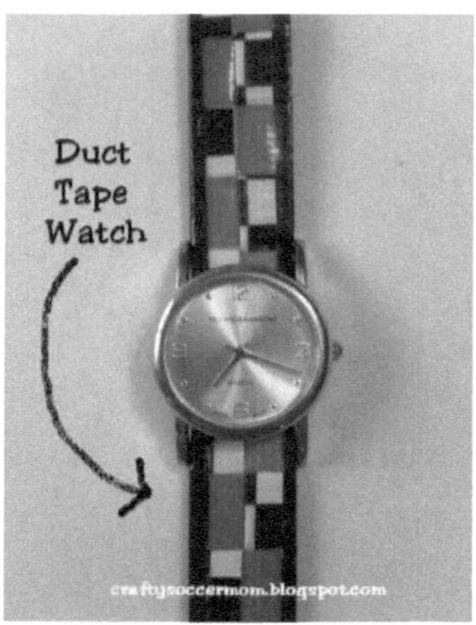

Materials

- Patterned duct tape
- Scissors
- Sewing thread
- Needle
- Old watch strap

Directions

1. Cut a piece of duct tape, double the length of the watchstrap without the buckle on it and, if necessary, cut them lengthwise so that they will fit through the watch pins.

2. Thread half of the first strip through the watch pin, and then fold the duct tape over so that the sticky sides are facing and that there are no sticky bits left exposed. Trim using the watchstrap as a template to get the shape right, and use the needle to punch holes in the duct tape so that you can fasten the buckle.

3. Pick up the watchstrap with the buckle and use it to measure out a second piece of duct tape. This piece should be double the length of the strap without the buckle. Add on an extra inch.

4. Trim the strap so that it will fit through the watch pin and thread it through. Thread through the extra inch as well and then stick the two sides together. You should now have an inch of adhesive exposed on the underside of the watchstrap.

5. Taper the watchstrap using the previous one as a template and then remove the buckle. Thread the buckle onto the sticky end of your strap, bringing it right up to the spot where the doubled strap begins. Fold the adhesive side down to enclose the bar of the buckle.

33. Duct Tape Bath Toy

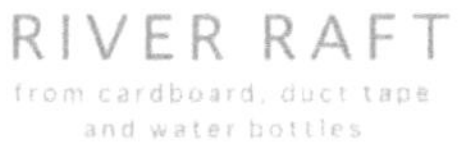

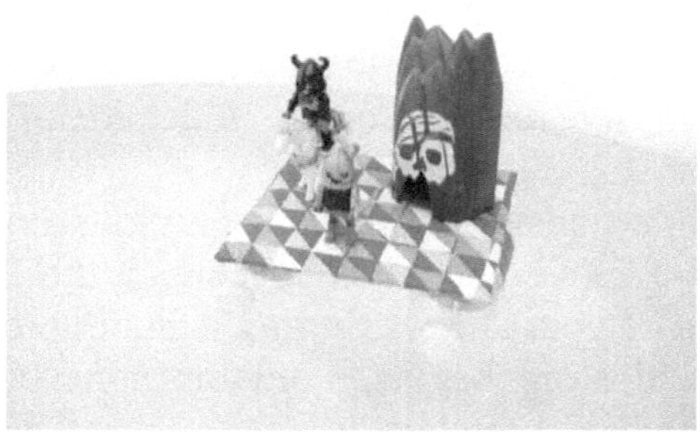

Materials

- Duct tape in colors of your choice
- 2 empty water bottles (the larger the bottles, the larger the toy)
- A square of cardstock to act as a raft

Directions

1. Cover the cardstock with duct tape; you can make patterns if you like. Just make sure that no cardstock shows through at the end.

2. Attach the water bottles to the underside of the cardstock using duct tape, and reinforce them with more tape.

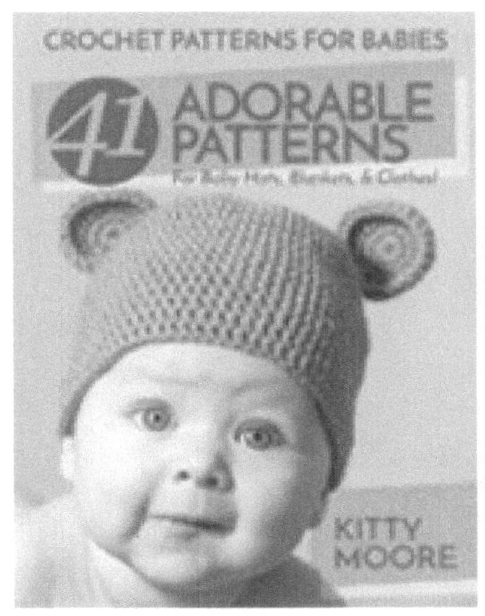

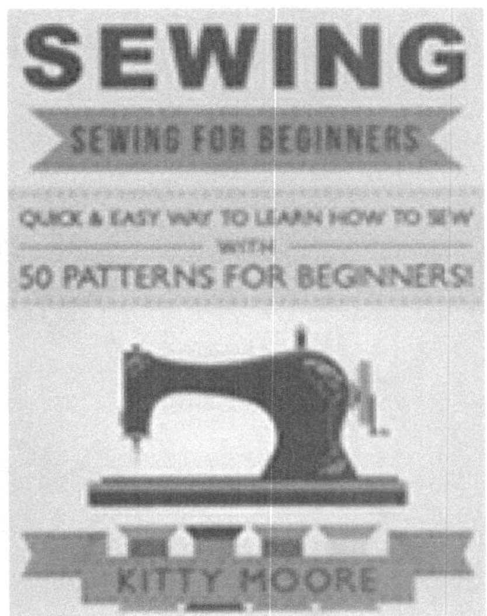

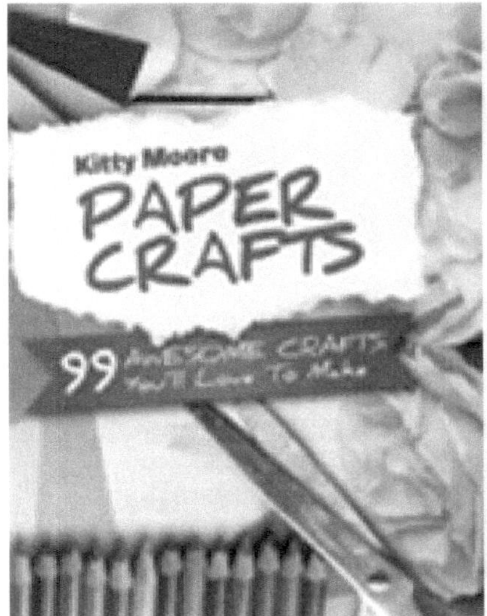

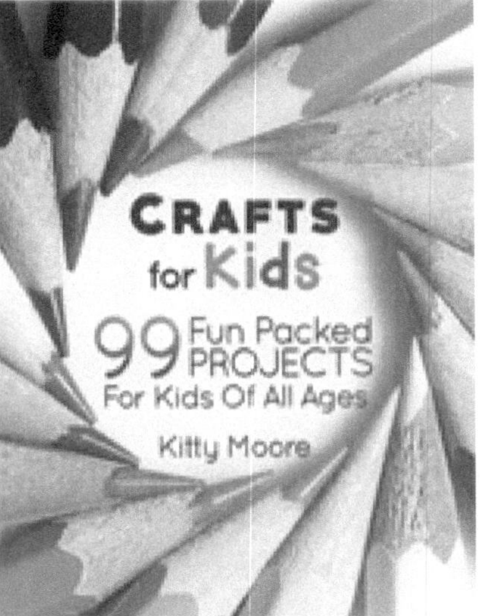

Check out Kitty's books at:

ArtsCraftsAndMore.com/go/books

34. Duct Tape Pouch

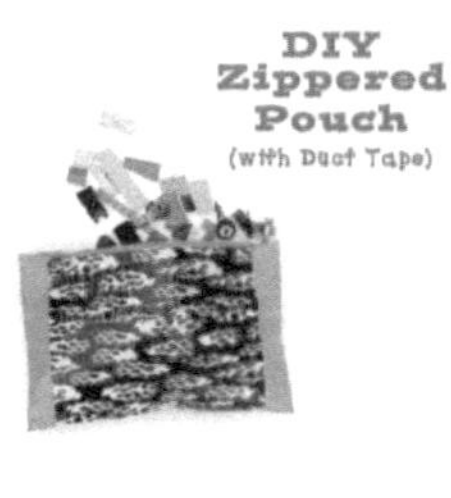

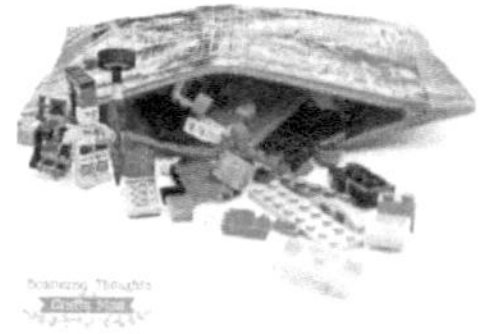

Materials

- 7-inch zipper
- Duct tape in colors of your choice
- Hot glue gun and glue
- Craft knife or scissors
- A ruler

Directions

1. Cut a few strips of duct tape. Each should be about 11 inches long. Lay the first sticky side up and lay the second on top, overlapping by about a quarter inch. Continue until your square measures 11 inches by 11 inches.

2. Once your "fabric" is the right size, repeat the process, this time laying the strips sticky side down. There should be no adhesive edges showing now. Trim so that the outside edges are straight.

3. Fold in half and crease well. The zipper will be placed on the top open end of the pouch. Measure an inch from the stopper of the zipper and trim down both of the outer short edges.

Cut one length of duct tape 10.5 inches long, and fold each of the edges to the middle of the tape.

4. Fold this in half again so that it creases well. This gives a clean look and will allow the neat application of the zipper. Make a second piece in the same manner. Set the zipper on a flat surface face down. On the outside edge of the zipper, apply your hot glue in a thin line.

5. Open up one of your pieces made in the step above and press the inside edge onto the zipper. Turn the zipper over and glue down the other edge. Repeat on the opposite side of the zipper with the second piece made. Make sure that all joints are secure.

6. Place the enclosed zipper, topside down. Cut one more 11-inch piece of tape, and apply it to the underside of the zipper casing. There should be at least a quarter inch overlap of tape so there will be some adhesive tape showing. Repeat on the opposite side.

7. Now you need to attach the adhesive edges to the inner edges of the pouch that you made. Check the outside of the pouch for stray bits of glue. If there are any, carefully remove them using the craft knife. Trim the tape so that it fits exactly.

8. Now you want to seal the sides. Cut two pieces of duct tape 6 inches in length each. Lay these pieces sticky side up on your surface. Mark the midpoint of each strip.

9. Place the midpoint of one of the short edges of the pouch onto the midpoint of the tape, making sure that there is an overlap of at least a quarter inch lengthwise. Fold the short edges of the tape down onto both sides to create a neat look before folding the tape in half lengthwise to seal the joint. Flip and repeat to reinforce the joint, and then follow the same steps on the other short edge. Trim any excess as necessary. Reinforce as required.

35. Kiddies' Laptop

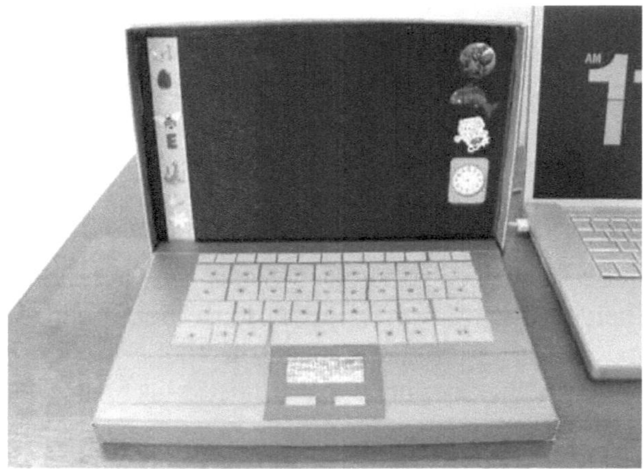

Materials

- 2 Shoebox lids
- Duct tape in silver and black
- Black acrylic paint
- Stick on letters and numbers
- Stickers that your kid will like

Directions

1. Paint the inside and outside of both shoebox lids black and set them aside to dry.

2. Your "keyboard" will be made from the outside of one shoebox lid and should be covered in silver duct tape.

3. Mark out the keys in black tape or a color of your choice. Affix the letters and numbers using your computer keyboard as a guide. Mark out a square to represent the laptop mouse pad.

4. The screen will be made using the inside of the other shoebox lid. Place stickers on the "screen" so that they look like the icons of your computer. On the outside of your "screen," place another sticker that looks like the logo of a computer company.

5. Secure the keyboard and screen together on the backside with duct tape. You can now open and close your "laptop".

36. Duct Tape Storage Boxes

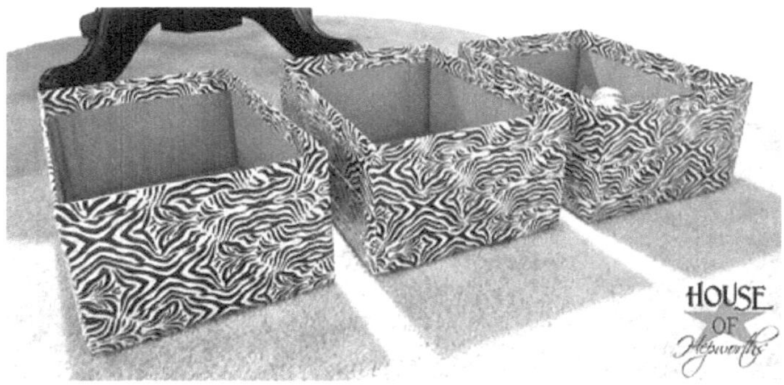

Materials

- Shoe boxes or shipping boxes without the top flaps
- Patterned duct tape
- Embellishments as desired
- A hot glue gun

Directions

1. Make sure that all top edges of the boxes are even. Trim with a craft knife in need.

2. Attach a piece of duct tape at the bottom edge of the box and work your way around until that level is completely covered. Repeat until the whole box is covered in duct tape, taking it right up to over the rim of the box.

3. Embellish as desired with the hot glue gun.

37. Duct Tape Tissue Box

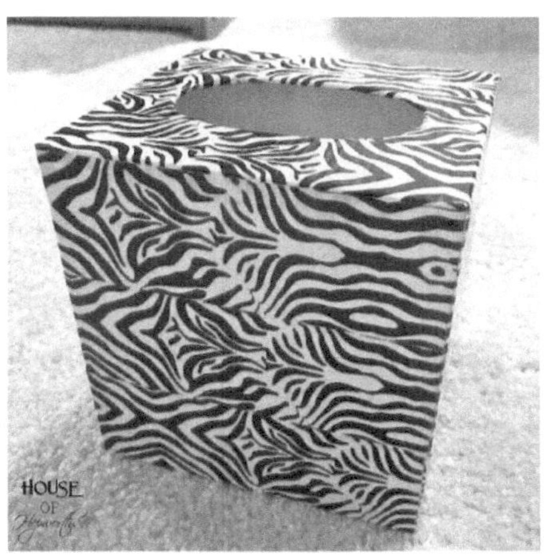

Materials

- An old tissue box that needs brightening up
- Patterned duct tape
- A craft knife

Directions

1. Follow the procedure as detailed above, this time covering the top of the box as well, until you actually get to the opening.

2. The opening is a little bit trickier – Place your strips as normal but cut small triangles out of the pieces that overhang the opening in order to make it easier for them to follow the curve when affixing them to the opening of the box.

38. Revamped Mirror

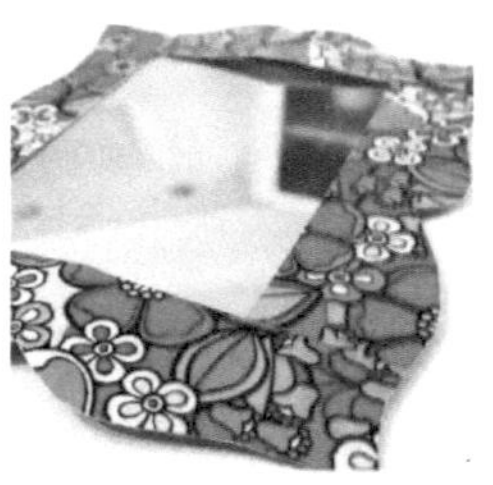

Materials

- Scissors or a craft knife
- Mirror
- Stiff cardstock
- Patterned Duct Tape
- Pencil
- Ruler
- Strong glue

Directions

1. Lay the mirror on the cardstock, and trace around it. Draw a frame within these lines that is at least a quarter inch smaller. You need this to glue the cardstock to. Cover the frame with duct tape, making sure that the ends are concealed at the back of the frame.

2. Draw your outer frame or download a template to help you do this. The border can be as wide as you like. Once you are happy with the shape, cut the cardstock. Glue the frame onto the front of the mirror and hang it in your house.

39. Customized Lanyard

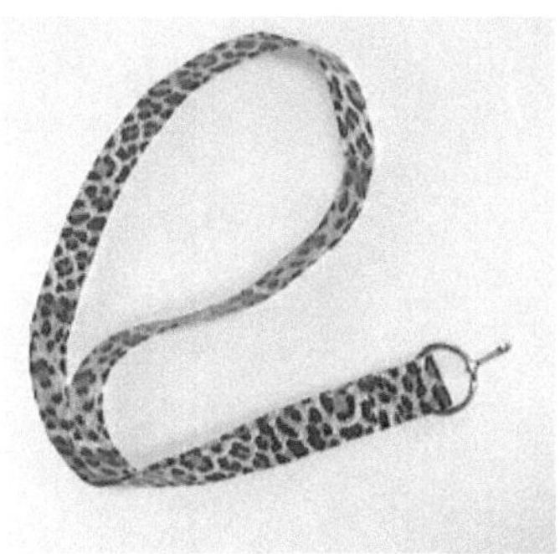

Materials

- Scissors
- Patterned duct tape
- Lanyard fitting
- Key ring

Directions

1. Cut a long length of duct tape (at least 30"). Then, fold it in half lengthwise with the sticky sides facing.

2. Thread onto the key ring and join up the loose ends using another strip of tape. Cut a short 2-inch piece of tape and cut it down until it is only a quarter inch wide.

3. Fold the lanyard in half, and tie a piece about 2 inches from the key ring using this strip. Put the lanyard fitting on.

40. Glasses Case

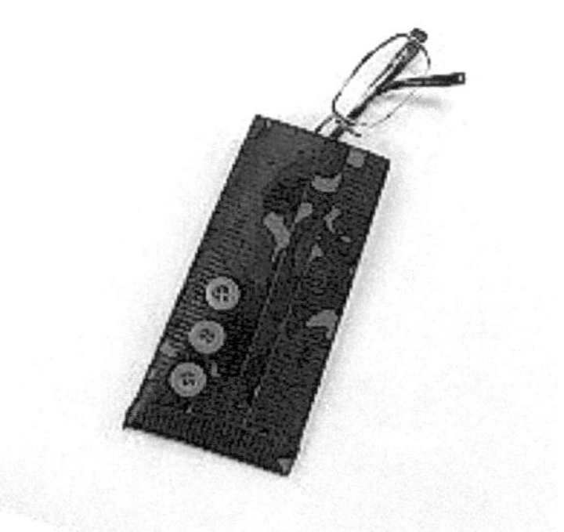

Materials

- Patterned duct tape
- Tacky adhesive
- Scissors
- Embellishments of your choice
- Craft foam

Directions

1. Cut the foam to a square 7 inches by 7 inches, and cover both sides with the duct tape.

2. Fold this in half. Close off two of the sides, leaving one of the short sides open. Trim as necessary.

3. Glue on whatever embellishments you want.

41. Extra Seating

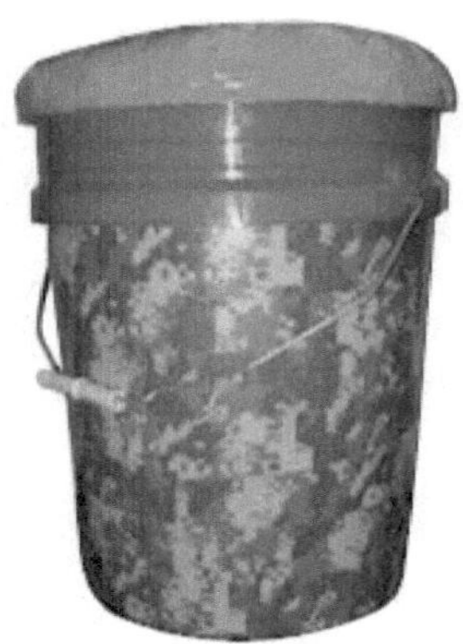

Materials

- A sturdy pail (it should be able to support some weight and big enough to use as a seat)
- Dense foam
- Patterned or plain duct tape
- A craft knife

Directions

1. Wrap your duct tape around the outside of the pail making sure it is smooth. Create patterns on the pail if you like. Using the lid as a template cut the foam so that it fits onto the lid of the pail snugly.

2. Tape the foam in place using the duct tape and cover all the foam with the tape. Be careful not to tape the lid down; you still want to be able to open and close the pail.

3. Trim the ends as necessary for a neat finish and cut two small slits in the top so that air is able to escape whenever weight is added to the seat. The great part of this is that it makes an excellent storage container and a seat as well.

42. Portable Cushion

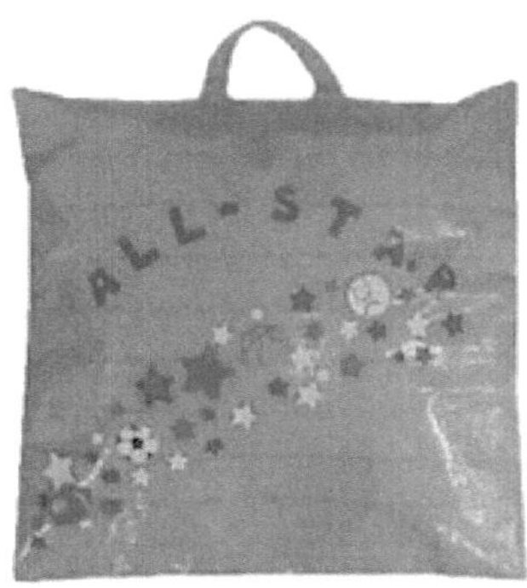

Materials

- Patterned or plain duct tape
- A square pad of foam
- Scissors
- Embellishments of your choice
- Glue

Directions

1. Measure your foam pad. Add this measurement to the depth of the foam pad and a further 2 inches. This will be the measurement used to cut the duct tape.

2. Lay your first strip adhesive side up on a flat surface. Lay the second, overlapping the first by a quarter of an inch. Continue until you have a square of duct tape with equal sides. Repeat, this time placing the duct tape adhesive side down so that no adhesive bits are showing.

3. Make a second piece of fabric in the same manner. Trim the edges of both sheets so that they are straight. Cut a piece of duct tape 18 inches long and fold it over lengthwise with the adhesive sides facing so that no adhesive sides are facing.

4. Attach to one of the pieces of "fabric" using duct tape. Make sure that it is secure. Lay the second sheet of "fabric" on top of the first and tape the edges of the other three sides together using strips of tape.

5. Put the foam in and then close up the fourth side. Staple the handles to reinforce them before sealing up the edge with duct tape. Embellish as desired.

43. Cute and Easy Hair Clips

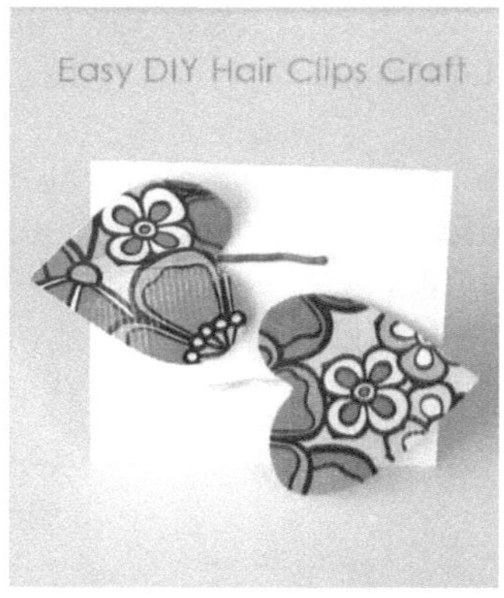

Living Locurto.com

Materials

- Pretty patterned duct tape
- Bobby pins
- Scissors
- Nail varnish in matching colors
- Cardstock

Directions

1. Slide the bobby pins onto the cardstock and paint them using the varnish. Set them aside to dry.

2. Cut a piece of duct tape about 4 inches in length and fold it over so that the sticky sides are inside. Cut out heart shapes or any shape that you like.

3. Cut a piece of tape about ½ an inch long. Slide this piece into the bobby pin, adhesive side facing up. Attach the heart to this strip, and you are all done.

44. Pencil Roll

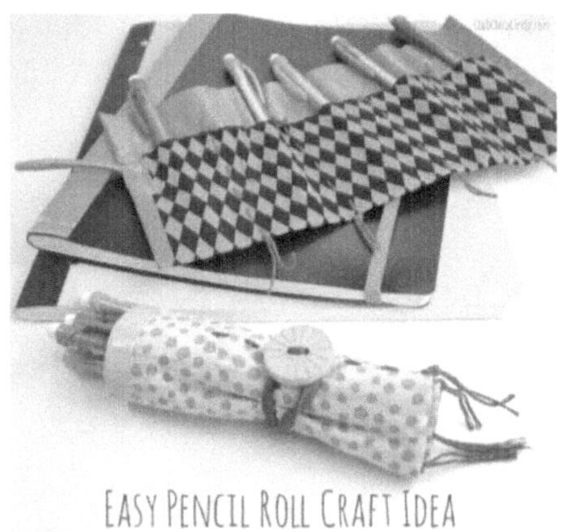

EASY PENCIL ROLL CRAFT IDEA

Materials

- Coordinating duct tape in colors of your choice
- Scissors
- A rotary cutter and mat
- Ruler
- A big pretty button
- A hair band

Directions

1. Cut strips of duct tape in your first color 10 inches long. Lay your first strip adhesive side up on a flat surface. Lay the second strip slightly overlapping the previous one, and repeat until your sheet measures 8.25 inches by 10 inches.

2. Repeat this procedure, this time laying the duct tape with the adhesive side facing down so that no adhesive is exposed. Create a second sheet in the same manner, this time making it 5 inches by 10 inches. Line up the bottom and short edges of the sheet and tape into place with more duct tape.

3. Sew the divisions for the pencils using your needle and thread. At the inside left edge of your roll, secure the hairgrip using duct tape. Roll up the roll so that you can place the button correctly and then sew the button into place.

45. Fun Duct Tape Boats

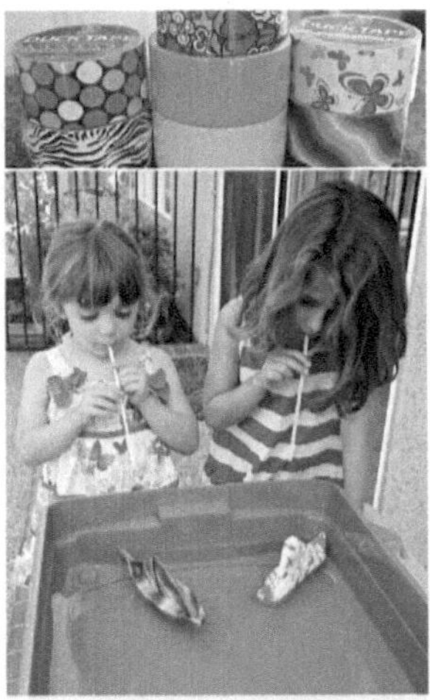

Duck Tape® **Boat Races**

Materials

- Patterned or colorful duct tape
- Paper measuring 8 ½ inches by 11 inches
- Scissors
- A large bowl of water and straws for trying out the boats

Directions

1. Lay your paper out flat and cover with the tape. Flip and cover the other side as well. No paper should show through at all. Fold the paper in half lengthwise.

2. Fold in half widthwise to find the center point. Take the top corners, where the folds are, and fold these to the center point you have created. They will form a triangle and there will be a bit left over at the bottom consisting of the open edges.

3. Fold the top edge up so that they cover the bottom of the triangle. Flip and repeat with the other flap. Gently open up

the "hat" that you have created. Bring the two outer edges of
your hat together so that they meet and flatten.

4. Fold the corners up around about an inch or so. Grasp to two
   ends and pull them out to form the shape of your boat. Fold
   up the bottom edge so that you have a proper boat shape.
   Secure the ends of the boat using more tape.

46. Duct Tape Embellished Table Runner

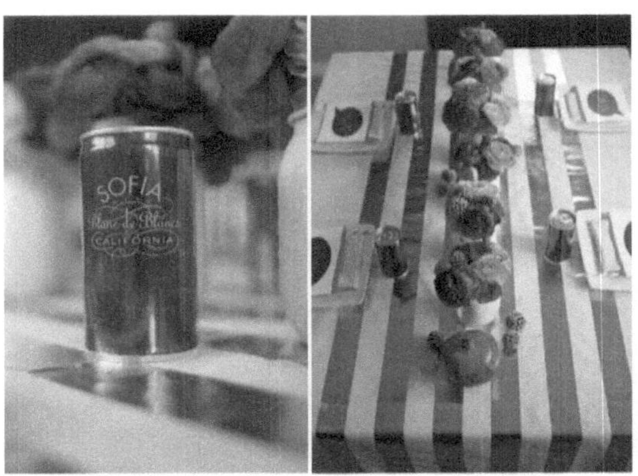

Materials

- A plain linen tablecloth
- Duct tape in a contrasting color – metallic is really great
- A craft knife
- Measuring tape

Directions

1. Measure your tablecloth lengthwise and cut strips of duct tape that can be laid along this length. Lay it carefully so that there are no bubbles. It is best to do this on a flat surface. Use as many lines of tape as you like. You can even play with using different widths of the same color tape.

2. When you get bored with it, just pull it off the tablecloth.

47. Create Your Own Wall Art

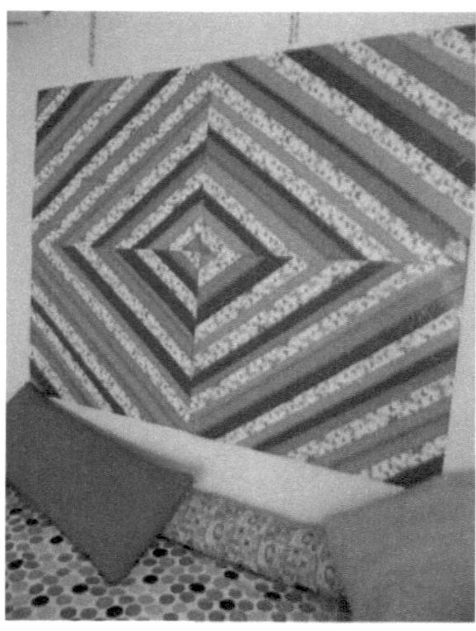

Materials

- An artist's canvas as big as you like
- Various patterned and plain duct tape in the colors that you like
- A craft knife
- A small piece of cardstock
- A pencil and ruler

Directions

1. Plan out your design on the cardstock first so that you can see whether or not it works. With duct tape, simple, straight-edged geometric shapes work really well.

2. When you're happy, mark out your design on the artist's canvas. Apply the duct tape according to the design you came up with. The ends should be tucked over the side of the canvas and hidden at the back. Trim the edges as required. Make sure all pieces are smooth.

48. Revamped Chair

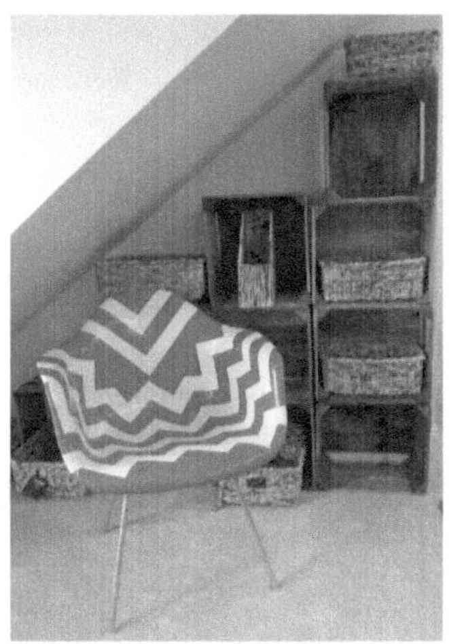

Materials

- A plastic or wooden chair in need of some brightening up
- Duct tape in two contrasting colors
- A pencil and ruler

Directions

1. Start by covering your chair in your background color of duct tape. Make sure to smooth out any bubbles as necessary.

2. Mark out your chosen design using the pencil and ruler. Aim for straight edges and bold shapes. Curves do not work as well when it comes to duct tape. Lay in your design using the second layer of duct tape.

49. Duct Tape Pencil Toppers

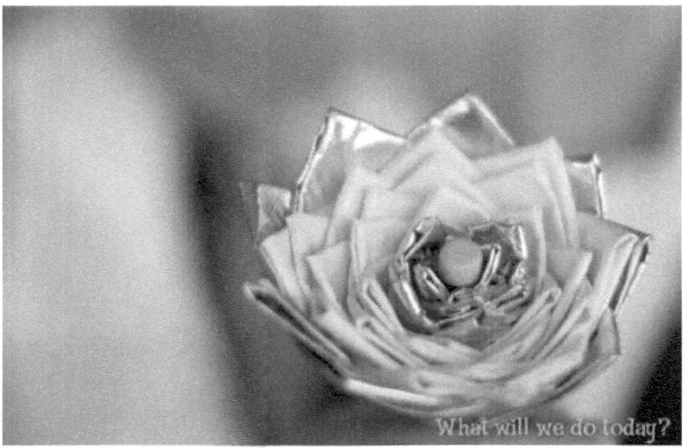

Materials

- Duct tape in the colors of your choice
- Scissors or a craft knife
- Pencils
- Duct tape in green

Directions

1. Cut a number of different pieces of duct tape about 2 inches long. You want a rectangular piece of duct tape. Cut a lot of pieces, and tape them down to the edge of a plastic board to keep them ready for use

2. Place your first piece sticky side up and fold the bottom right corner on the long edge up towards the middle. There should be about an eighth of an inch space at the top edge. The side edge left uncovered will be wider.

3. Now fold up the other side so that you end up with a pentagon shape. At this stage, the only adhesive side showing should be at the bottom.

4. Wrap the sticky edge around that base of your pencil. Repeat this procedure, placing each petal next to the previous one with a slight overlap until your flower is full enough.

5. Once done, wrap the green tape around the base of the petals and pencil so that it looks like a stem.

50. Rosy Rings

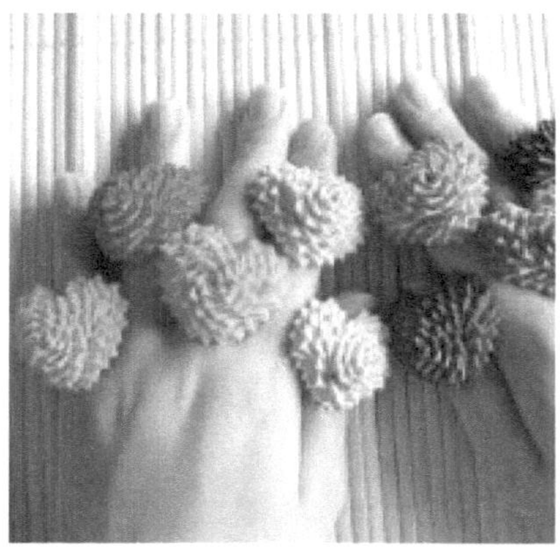

Materials

- Duct tape in the colors of your choice
- Scissors or a craft knife

Directions

1. Measure the circumference of your finger and cut a strip of tape that is about an inch longer than this. Fold over on itself to form your ring base.

2. Now proceed as you did in the tutorial for the pencil toppers, this time wrapping the sticky edges around the tip of the ring. The extra inch gets pinched in to give you a base for your flower and to close it off.

51. Creative Calla Lilies

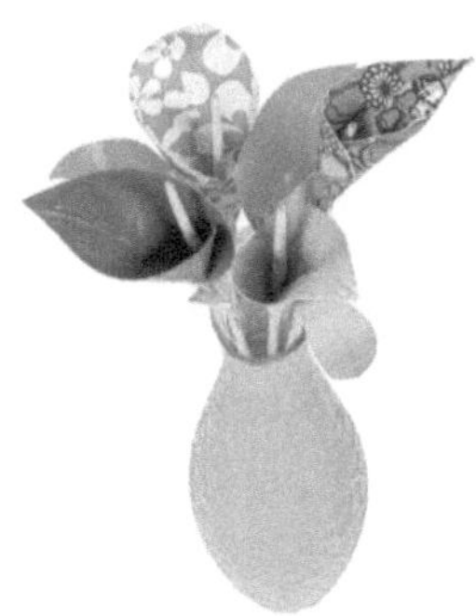

Materials

- Craft knife or scissors
- Duct tape in a range of prints and colors
- Florist's wire
- A pen or pencil
- Wire cutters
- Dowelling rods for stems

Directions

1. Cut a 4-inch strip of yellow duct tape and cut the strip in halfway from the bottom left corner to the top right corner so the resulting shape is triangular.

2. Cover the rest of the "stem" with green duct tape.

3. Cut two more 4-inch pieces of duct tape and lay them sticky side up, overlapping a little.

4. Cut a 4-inch length of floral wire and place in the center of your "fabric." Cut two more strips of tape and lay them over the first so that none of the adhesive is exposed.

5. Draw the shape of your calla lily petal, using the tip of the wire as the central highest point.

6. Cut the petal out and secure in place using a smaller strip of duct tape. You need to roll the bottom of the petal to form the correct shape.

7. Cut your teardrop out using your scissors. This will be the large petal. Repeat these steps for each lily.

52. Duct Tape Gift Envelope

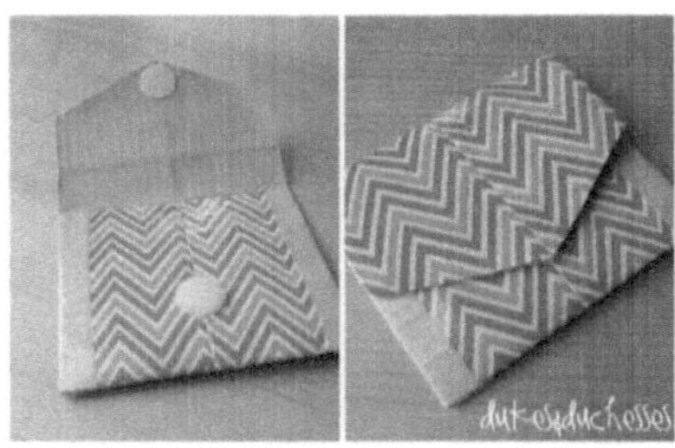

Materials

- Patterned duct tape
- Plain duct tape in a matching color
- Velcro
- Hot glue gun

Directions

1. Cut strips of the patterned tape 12 inches long. Lay the first strip sticky side up and lay the next on top with an overlap. Continue until your "fabric" is 5 inches wide.

2. Cut an equal number of strips in the plain tape and lay them sticky side down over your first piece of "fabric" so that no adhesive bits are exposed.

3. Fold into thirds along the length of the "fabric" so that the patterned tape is on the outside. The first two thirds will form the envelope itself; the last third will be the flap.

4. Shape the flap so that it is more triangular shape. Cut two 4-inch lengths of plain tape and use them to seal the side seams of your envelope.

5. Cut your Velcro into a small circle and affix one half to the inside of the envelope flap and the other half to the outside of the envelope.

53. Duct Tape Frame

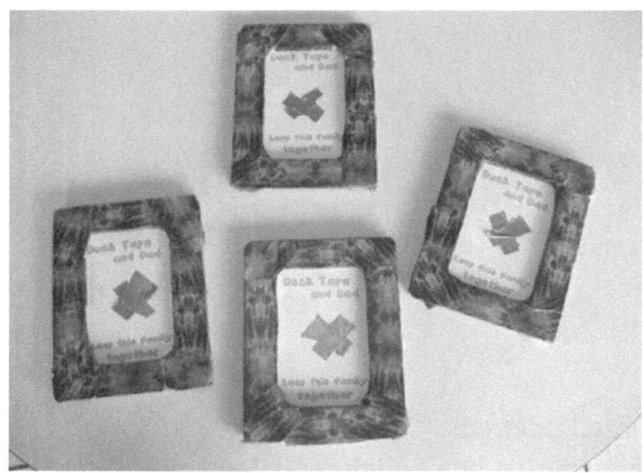

Materials

- Duct tape in your choice of patterns and colors
- A cheap frame or frame that needs a revamp
- A craft knife

Directions

1. There are a few basic ways of approaching this project, all of which give great results. You can simply choose plain duct tape in contrasting colors to give a great finish or you can choose one patterned tape or a combination of the two.

2. Cover the frame with duct tape, making sure that any edges are at the back. Trim to neaten and you are done.

54. Duct Tape Rose Petal Necklace

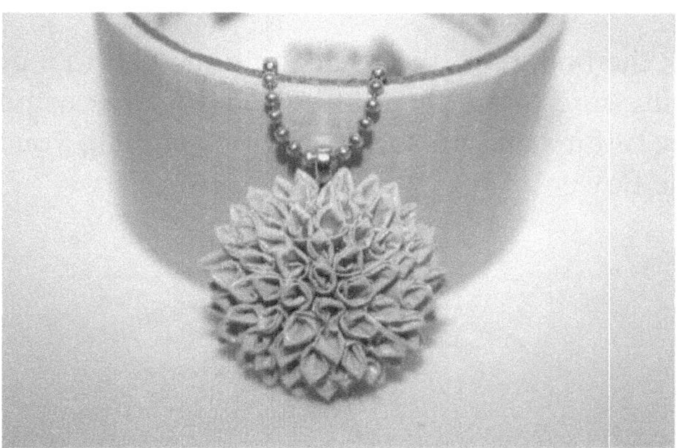

Materials

- Duct tape
- Hot glue gun
- A pair of scissors
- Neck chain with clip

Directions

1. Fold a corner of the tape halfway covering the width side. Fold in the corner of the remaining centimeter to make a triangle on the topside of your tape. The triangle should be the color of the duct tape and the remaining part should be the sticky side.

2. Fold even smaller strips of the duct tape, this time length-wise on the sticky side. The small triangle will look like the petal top and the bottom part some short stems.

3. Use your scissors to cut your stems into six pieces. Cut a 3 cm by 5 cm duct tape strip and roll it into a ball. Cut another thinner strip and roll it around the ball to ensure no sticky section is still out. Repeat if the strip of tape in not enough.

4. Taking care not to burn yourself, use the hot glue gun to put hot glue on one side of your ball.

5. Stick the bottom of the petals onto the ball in a circular way, making sure to put them as closely together as possible. The shape of the ball will shape your flower. Clip your neck chain to the flower.

55. Duct Tape Tote

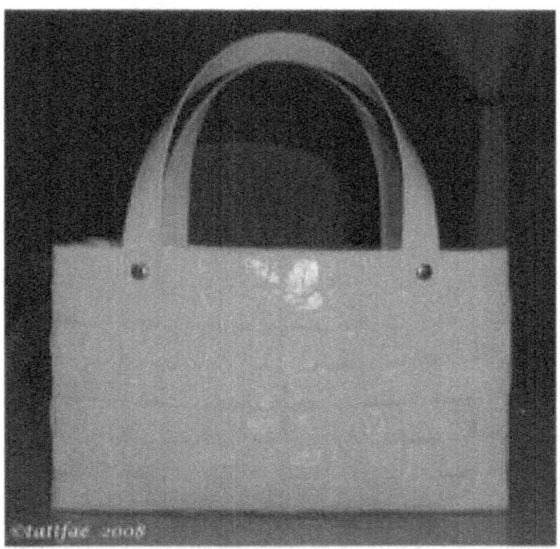

Materials

- Duct tape (one or two different colors)
- Scissors
- Staple gun
- Ruler
- Marker

Directions

1. Cut twelve 15-inch strips of duct tape. You will also need 24 10-inch strips. Lay one 15-inch strip on a level surface sticky side up. Fold the tape in such a way that the two longer sides meet at the center.

2. Do the same for all twelve of them and for the 10-inch ones as well. Set six of the 15-inch strips next to each other so they are touching. Take one 10-inch and weave it into the 15-inch ones by letting it go under the first 15-inch strip, then on top, under, on top and so on until you reach the last strip.

3. Your second 10-inch strip should then start on top, then under, on top, under etc. until the end. Repeat this with twelve of them to give you one side of your bag. Line that

side preferably with clear tape by laying the tape in 15-inch strips along the length of that first side and letting the strips slightly overlap so that the outside color will not show from inside.

4. Cut another 15-inch strip and fold it half in and half out the length of the top of your bag part to smoothen it. Repeat steps. Hold the two sides facing each other, outer part in. Use a staple gun to closely staple the edges of the two sides together. Cut two duct tape strips the width of your bag and one the length.

5. Place the shorter tapes on the sides of your bag, half on the stapled section and half off. Fold the remaining sticky part together with the stapled part so that the joint lies flat against the side. Repeat using the longer strip for the bottom of your bag.

6. Place your bag bottom down and press down the bottom corners from outside and staple the triangular corner edge about 2 inches from the end. Fold down the two triangular edges under the bag and cover them and the entire bottom with duct tape for durability.

7. Push the bottom in to turn your bag inside out and pull out the bottom corners properly. To make the handles, cut two 20-inch long strips of duct tape and fold them as in step 2.

8. Bend each of these into an arc, and tape both ends of each 2-3 inches from the side. Make sure it is equidistant from both handles. Cover the taped handles with more tape going around the mouth of the bag for strength.

56. Duct Tape Garden Chair

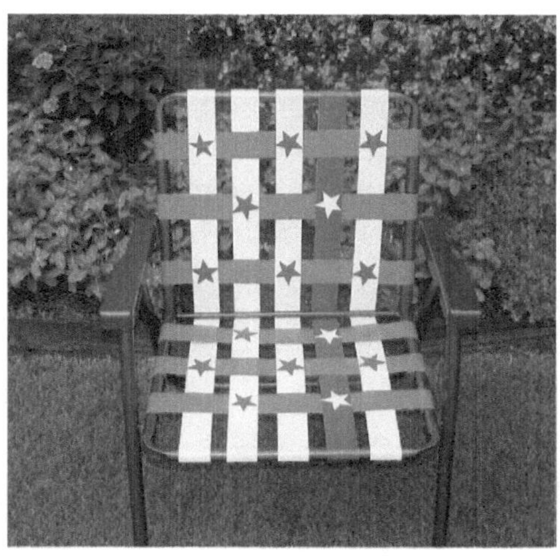

Materials

- Metal frame of old garden chair
- Duct tape (in colors of your choice)
- Tape measurer
- Scissors

Directions

1. Make sure the frame is clean. Measure the horizontal position you would put your duct tape and add an extra 4 inches to enable the tape to properly wrap around the frame.

2. Cut your first tape to the size you measured and place it on a flat surface sticky side down.

3. Cut and place three or four more on top of the first one, all facing down. The more you put, the stronger your chair will be. Remove tapes and place on the flat surface, now sticky side facing upwards.

4. Cut another duct tape strip to the same length short four inches and place it sticky side facing the first tape, to seal in the stickiness.

5. Leave two sticky inches on both sides of the tape. Carefully place the tape on the section of the frame you want it, allowing the sticky parts to circle the posts on both sides. Ensure it is tight, the tighter the better.

6. Repeat steps, placing the tape on different places but ensuring the tape is equidistant for the sturdiness of the chair.

7. When all the horizontal straps are in place, measure the length of the chair and repeat the steps again, this time weaving the tape through the horizontal straps and sticking to the post.

8. All the vertical straps should go under the bar at the back of the chair. Use a shape cutter of choice to cut shapes from the tape and put shapes or whatever you may want on your chair.

57. Gorgeous Duct Tape Clutch

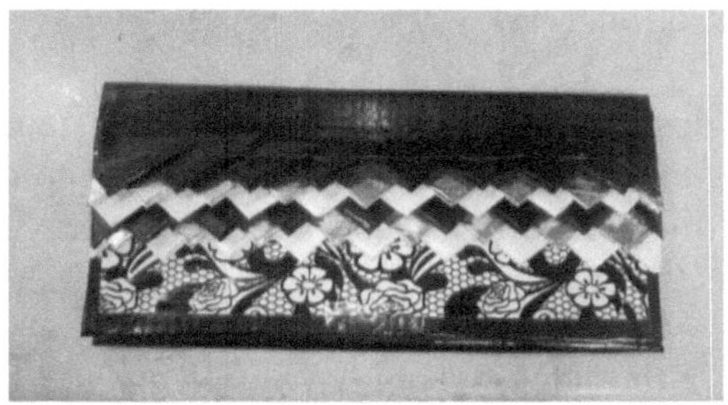

Materials

- Duct tape(s), color of choice
- Scissors
- Ruler

Directions

1. Cut a 10-inch strip of duct tape and place it sticky side down. Cut another one and place it sticky down, to slightly overlap with the first. Repeat step and place tape to slightly overlap with the last until that side measures up to 15 inches.

2. When you are done, you should have a width of 10 inches and a length of 15 inches. Turn the part you made so the sticky side faces up. Cut 15-inch strips and place them sticky side facing sticky side on the first part to completely cover any sticky part.

3. When you finish, both sides should not have any sticky sections Cut off any excess. Cut two 10-inch strips of duct tape and two 15-inch ones of a different but matching color if you like. Stick half the sticky part of any of them to the finished section all the length through.

4. Fold the remaining sticky part on the other side and repeat this with all the sides. Fold the length side into three equal

section of 5 inches and flatten the folded sections as best as you can. Use tape to stick together the sides of the first and second sections.

5. For the design, cut 2½ inch strips of duct tape, up to twenty of them. Put each strip sticky side up and fold one corner of the width flush to the other corner to leave a very small sticky section.

6. Fold over the sticky section you left by the side to turn the top part into a small triangle shape and leave the bottom section still sticky. Make several of these and place them side-by-side in a straight line length wise, about halfway on the third part of your clutch. The pointed part of you small triangles should face downward if your clutch is upright.

7. When you are done with the first row, cut an 8-inch tape and cut it in half, lengthwise. Carefully place this to cover the parts of the short tape strips you taped to the flip section of your clutch.

8. Place another row of small triangles as in the first, ensure the tip of the second rows of triangles is slightly behind the first and the tip is between two from the first row.

9. Repeat this until half the flip section of your clutch purse is covered. Put tape to cover the last row and you are done. Use magnetic clips for fastening the clutch closed.

58. Tri-Fold Duct Tape Handbag

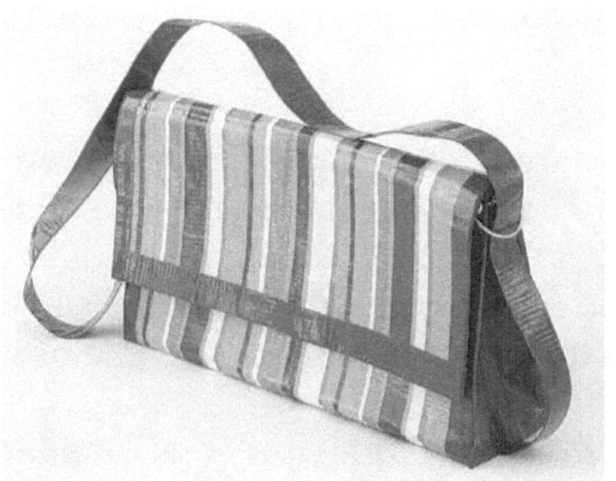

Materials

- Two duct tapes, matching colors
- Hard cardboard
- Pair of scissors
- Ruler and marker
- Staple gun and 2 D-rings

Directions

1. Cut off a 30-inch strip from one of the duct tapes and place it on a hard and flat surface sticky side up. Cut off another one and allow it to slightly overlap the first one, also sticky side up. Repeat step until the side you are working on is 15 inches long to give you a 30-inch by 15-inch side.

2. You can use the second duct tape to cut off same sized strips. Place the first one facing the first strip you put, sticky side to sticky side. Repeat step until all the sticky part is covered. Cut off the excess tape from the sides to make the sides straight.

3. Cut two 30-inch strips and two 15-inch ones and use them to smooth the ends of the fabric. Cut 16-inch strips of tape and tape them together as you did the first fabric, into a fabric 16

inches by 4 inches. Repeat steps to have two fabrics of the same size. Cut a 3-inch by 15-inch piece of cardboard and thoroughly cover it with duct tape so that no cardboard shows.

4. Place the larger duct tape fabric flat on the surface and measure 10 inches on the longer side. Place the cardboard across the fabric as if dividing the fabric into a 10-inch section and a 17-inch section. Use the staple gun to affix the cardboard to the fabric to make the base of your purse

5. Staple the shorter sides of the smaller fabrics to the cardboard, making sure the best side is on the outside then use duct tape to cover the staple pins. Pull the 10 inches you first measured and join them to the length of any of the smaller fabrics using staples, and then cover them with the tape. Repeat on the other side.

6. Now pull the ten inches of the other side and also staple them to the smaller fabrics to leave a side 7 inches long, this should be the flap of your bag. Place the bag on its side to make sure the pins on the inside seams are all covered with tape to avoid scratching. Fold and tape the top parts of the sides of the bag to reduce the length to an inch.

7. To make the handle, cut two 40-inch long strips of duct tape and lay the first on a level surface sticky side up. Fold the tape in such a way that the two longer sides meet at the center. Place the second on top and use it to wrap around the first.

8. Fold 2 3-inch pieces of tape in half lengthwise, and hook the D-rings. Place the open end of each strip on the top part of each of the sides of your bag and nicely tape it to hold together.

9. Pull the belt into one D-ring and tape the end of that side into position. Repeat on the other side to make your bag ready for use.

59. Duct Tape Redone High Heel Sandals

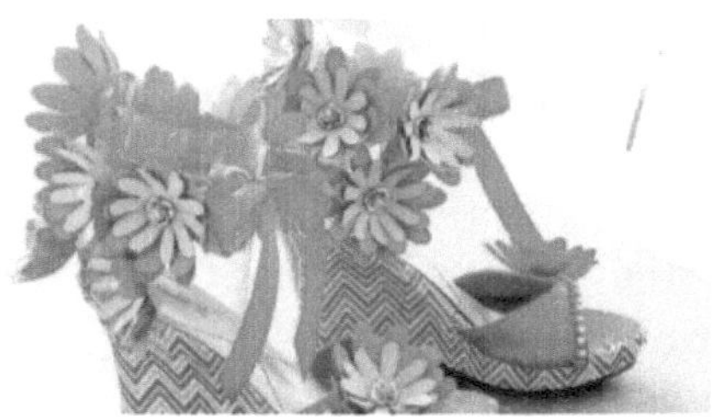

Materials

- Duct tapes
- Scissors
- Hot glue
- Old pair of shoes
- Artificial flowers of choice (if you do not want to make your own)

Directions

1. Let's start by making the flowers (start from step 11 if not making flowers. Cut squares of duct tape 1 inch by 1 inch

2. Fold in one corner of the square to leave a small section of sticky tape on two sides, fold the corresponding corner as well to make a small triangle with a section of sticky tape below. Make as many of these as you can using all the colors you need for your flowers.

3. Place a strip of duct tape sticky side down and cut circles of different sizes, starting with the smallest of radius ½ inch and adding ½ inch for the next size till you have four of them. Take three of the triangles you made in step 3 and join them together. A small hole will remain at the center.

4. Take the smallest of the circular tapes and tape more of the small triangles on the edge; there should be five of them

when you are done. Stick that circular tape with its triangles on the first ones you put together. Repeat steps ensuring the tips of the triangles form a pattern, until all your tape pieces are joined to the flower.

5. When you place you flower on a surface, ensure that only the tips of the triangles show. If not, trim any excess. Remove any decorations on your shoes and make sure they are clean. Starting with the heel, carefully tape on the preferred color duct tape. Make sure there are no creases. Cut and discard any creased tape.

6. Do the same for the top of the sandals until every part is how you want it. Use hot glue to glue the artificial flowers to the parts of your shoe you want highlighted.

7. Put back the parts you initially removed if you still want those or use more artificial flowers. Be as creative as you want with the artificial flowers as they give life to the shoe. The shoes are done once you are satisfied.

60. Woven Duct Tape Purse

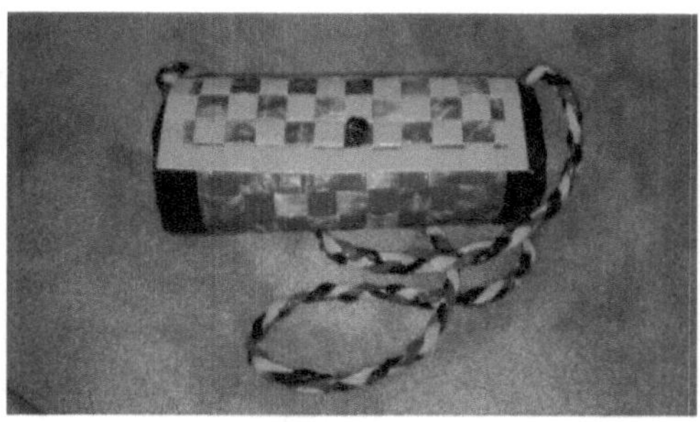

Materials

- Duct tape, two different colors
- Pair of scissors
- Staple gun
- Ruler
- Marker

Directions

1. Mark an area on a hard and flat surface to measure 10 by 20 inches. Cut a 20-inch strip of duct tape and place it on the 20-inch side, sticky side up. Fold the tape in such a way that the two longer sides meet at the center. Do the same for several more of the 20-inch ones and make 10-inch strips as well using a matching duct tape.

2. Set the 20-inch strips alongside each other, touching. Take one 10-inch strip and weave it into the 20-inch strips by letting it go under the first 20-inch strip, then on top, under, on top and so on till the sixth. Your second 10-inch strip should then start on top, then under, on top, under etc. Repeat this with enough of them to give you one 20 by 10-inch fabric.

3. Line that side preferably with clear tape by laying the tape in 20-inch strips along the length of that first side and letting the

strips slightly overlap so that the outside color will not show from inside. Cut 2 10-inch strips and fold them half in and half out of the shorter sides to smooth them. Cut 10-inch strips of tape and tape them together as you did the first fabric, into 2 pieces of fabric measuring 12 inches by 4 inches each.

4. Cut a 2-inch by 10-inch piece of cardboard and thoroughly cover it with duct tape so that no cardboard shows. Place the larger duct tape fabric flat on the surface and measure 6 inches on the longer side. Place the cardboard across the fabric as if dividing the fabric into a 6-inch section and a 12-inch section.

5. Use the staple gun to affix the cardboard to the fabric to make the base of your purse. Staple the shorter sides of the smaller fabrics to the cardboard, making sure the best side is on the outside then use duct tape to cover the staple pins.

6. Pull the 6 inches you first measured and join them to the length of any of the smaller fabrics using staples then cover with the tape. Repeat on the other side.

7. Now pull the 6 inches of the other side and also staple them to the smaller fabrics to leave a side also 6 inches long, this should be the flap of your purse. Place the purse on its side and ensure the pins on the inside seams are all covered with tape to avoid scratching.

8. To make the handle, cut three 35-inch long strips of duct tape, use the two colors of your purse and lay the first on a level surface sticky side up. Fold each tape in such a way that the two longer sides meet at the center then join the two sides.

9. Tape all three together on one end and braid them together then tape the other end as well to prevent running. Use pieces of tape to tape them into the smaller sides of your bag then tape the top side right round for strength.

61. Duct Tape Tri-Fold Wallet

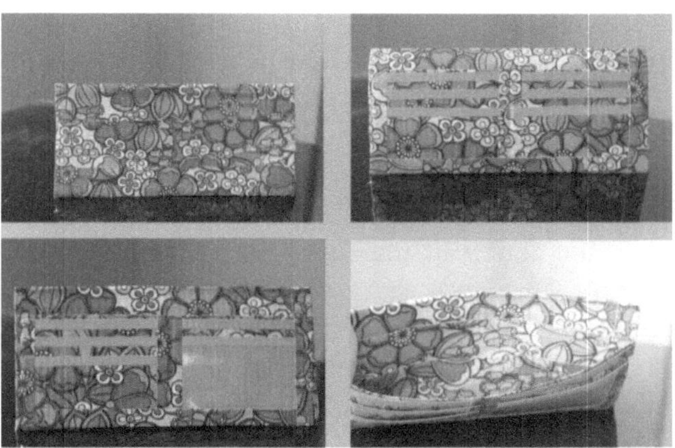

Materials

- Duct tape(s), color of choice one floral
- Scissors
- Ruler

Directions

1. Cut an 8-inch strip of the floral duct tape and place it sticky side down. Cut another one and place it sticky down, to slightly overlap with the first. Turn the part you made so the sticky side faces up. Cut strips and place them sticky side facing sticky side on the first part to completely cover any sticky part. When you finish, both sides should not have any sticky sections.

2. Cut off any excess to leave a fabric of 8 by 4 inches. Cut an 8-inch strip of duct tape of a different but matching color if you like. Stick half the sticky part of any of them to the finished section all the length through. Fold the remaining sticky part on the other side and repeat this with all the sides. Repeat steps.

3. Now use the same tape as you used for the inside of your wallet to make the card panels. Make 10 small fabrics, just over 3½ inches long and with widths of 2½ inches. Cut a strip of matching tape and cut it in half lengthwise. On the top part of 5 of the small fabrics, place the tape half in and half out to create a matching line.

4. Trim ½ inch from each of the remaining fabrics then place them at the center of the first 5 to leave 3 sides with a sticky side showing. Stick them on the inside of the first side of your wallet, side by side, right at the top. Leave a gap of ½ inch between the first panels and the second ones, which you should place just underneath. Leave same space and tape in the last one on one side of the wallet.

5. Create a clear panel using the steps above and using clear tape and tape it opposite the third panel, the clear one can serve as a, I.D. card panel.

6. Now tape together the two individual sides at the bottom and two sides with matching tape. Tape in a zip to the two sides to close that part. Place magnetic clips on the width part of the wallet and tape them over, they are for fastening the wallet closed.

62. Duct Tape Skirt & Blouse

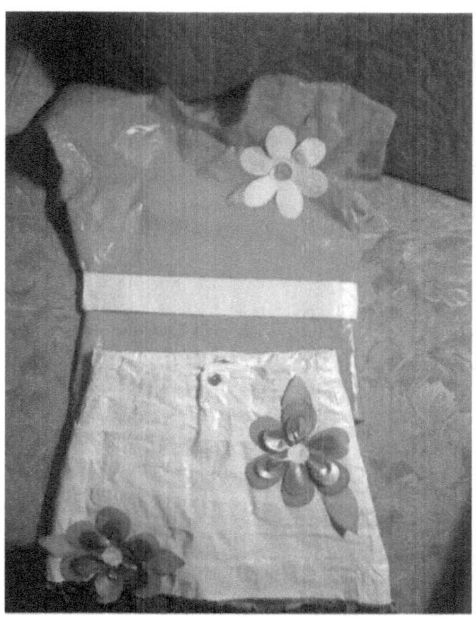

Materials

- Duct tapes of different colors
- Scissors
- Tape measure
- A zipper the height of the blouse
- Marker

Directions

1. Make your fabric by overlapping strips of duct tape then covering them with more duct tape to ensure all sticky parts are covered. The size you want for the clothes determines the lengths of your duct tape strips.

2. For the blouse, place the fabric on a flat surface and fold it so that the opening meets at the center.

3. Shape and cut the opening for the sleeves and collar. Tape the edges closed with a strip of tape. Tape the zipper in place for easy fitting. The zipper is the only joint, and it is at the back of the blouse.

4. Carefully tape a strip just above the waist and from one side of the zipper right around the blouse to the other side. Your blouse is finished. Repeat step to make the skirt.

5. Fold in the edges of the two height sides to make it smooth. Allow them to slightly overlap as you join them. Leave 3 inches on top for the buttons or whatever you will use to close it.

6. Adjust the waist, and tape the waistband into place.

7. Use another strip of tape to smooth the bottom part of your skirt. Cut six petal flower patterns using the left-over fabrics; make them different sizes and colors. Join 2 or 3 to make one flower until you have 3 flowers all together. Sew these onto the skirt and blouse to decorate them. Place the flowers where you want them, and you are done.

63. Pleated Duct Tape Purse

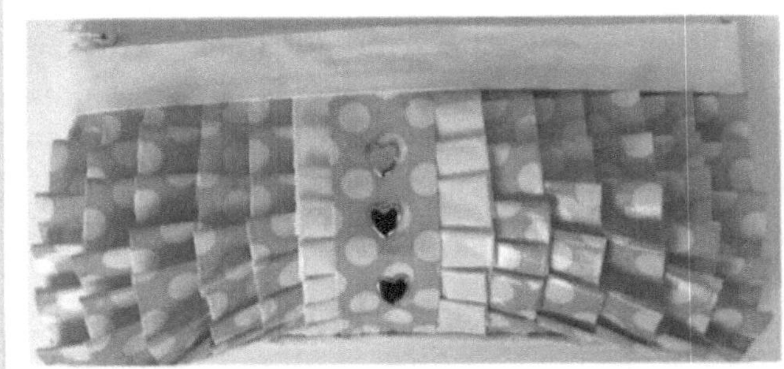

Materials

- Duct tape (in the color of your choice)
- Scissors
- Ruler
- Marker

Directions

1. Cut a 12-inch strip of duct tape and place it sticky side down. Cut another one and place it sticky down so that it slightly overlaps with the first. Continue this process until you have a piece that is 12 inches across.

2. When you are done, you should have a 12-inch by 12-inch piece. Turn the part you made so the sticky side faces up. Cut 12-inch strips and place them sticky side facing sticky side on the first part to completely cover any sticky part.

3. When you finish, neither side should have any sticky sections left. Cut off any excess duct tape. Cut two 12-inch strips of duct tape of a different but coordinating color if you like. Stick half the sticky part on one side of your fabric.

4. Fold the remaining sticky part on the other side and repeat this with the opposite side. Cut a long strip of matching tape

and fold it in half lengthwise. Cut another 12-inch strip, and tear it into three pieces. Then place it sticky side up.

5. Make same size pleats with the longer tape and tape the pleats with the 12-inch strips leaving a section of the pleated tape still sticky. Cut it when it's 12 inches long and repeat to make a second strip. Stick them onto the fabric facing each other, leaving only 3 inches between them at the center.

6. Tear another 12-inch duct tape strip into two and tape one of them between the two pleated tapes to hide where they are taped to the bag. Repeat steps and then lift the un-taped end of the first pleat to tape in the second pleat on one side and then the other. Repeat step until the whole fabric is covered.

7. Use the same tape you used for the first line of pleats to stick half the sticky part on one side of your fabric covering the pleats on the edges. Do this on opposite sides to make that the opening of your bag.

8. Now fold your fabric into two equal parts to make a pocket with the pleats inside. Tape together the sides to form your purse making sure not to tape the pleats as well. Turn it inside out and glue in some golden or silver buttons at the center of the pleats and you have your beautiful pleated purse.

64. Duct Tape Handbag & Matching Shoes

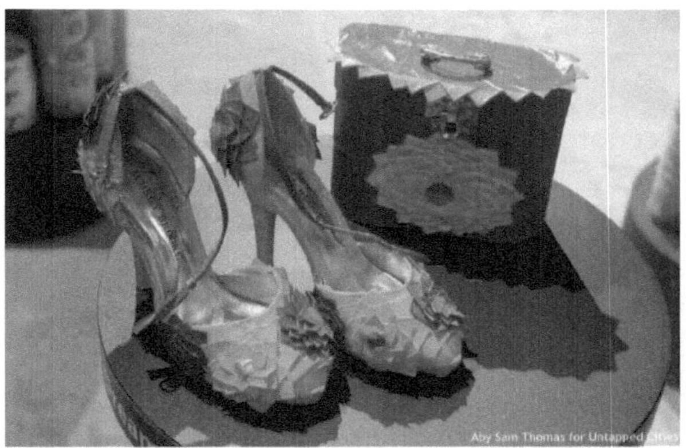

Materials

- Duct tapes
- Scissors
- Hot glue
- Old pair of shoes
- Old handbag

Directions

1. Let's start by making the flowers. Cut squares of duct tape into 1-inch by 1-inch squares. Fold in one corner of the square to leave a small section of sticky tape on two sides, fold the corresponding corner as well to make a small triangle with a section of sticky tape below. Make as many of these as you can using all the colors you need for your flowers.

2. Place a strip of duct tape sticky side down and cut circles of different sizes, starting with the smallest of radius ½ inch and adding ½ inch for the next size until you have four of them. Take three of the triangles you made in step 3, and join them together. A small hole will remain at the center.

3. Take the smallest of the circular tapes and tape more of the small triangles on the edge; there should be five of them when you are done. Stick that circular tape with its triangles on the first ones you put together. Repeat steps ensuring the tips of the triangles form a pattern, until all your pieces of tape are joined to the flower.

4. When you place you flower on a surface, ensure that only the tips of the triangles show, if not, trim any other pieces showing. Close the top of the flower by gluing a matching button. Now remove any decorations from your shoes and handbag.

5. Remove any dirt or dust they may have. Start with the shoe heal and carefully tape on the preferred color duct tape. Remove creases carefully. Do the same for the top of the shoes until every part is fully covered.

6. Use hot glue to glue the artificial flowers to the front and backsides of the shoes. Carefully put tape around the belt strips with a matching or same color as you already used. The handbag is much simpler as you tape around it using duct tape color preferably matching the one you put on the shoes. Duct tape the inside of the bag as well.

7. For the lid of the bag, use the same small triangles as the ones used to make the flowers and tape them on the edge from inside. Use more tape to cover the inside of the lid and keep the triangles in place. Make a slightly bigger flower with colors that match the shoes and place this on one side of the handbag.

65. Duct Tape Earrings

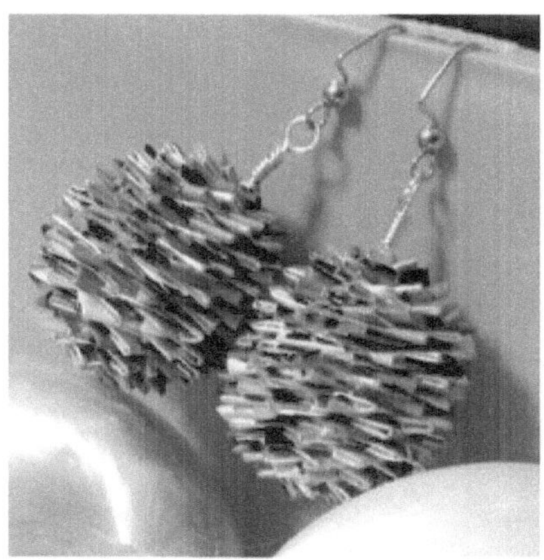

Materials

- Duct tapes of varying colors
- Scissors or precision knife
- Earring hooks
- Hot glue gun

Directions

1. Cut squares of duct tape 1-inch by 1-inch. Fold in one corner of the square to leave a small section of sticky tape on two sides, fold the corresponding corner as well to make a small triangle with a section of sticky tape below.

2. Make as many of these as you can using all the colors you need for your earrings.

3. Take one of the small triangles and fold it over itself to save as the base for our craft and the inner part of the rose.

4. Take a different colored one and paste it on, ensuring the tip is on a different side.

5. Keep adding these small triangles in the same manner, alternating the colors. Repeat until the rose can rest comfortably on its base. Repeat steps until you have similar roses.

6. Tape your earring hook to one of the base petals and place the two bases facing each other.

7. Glue the two bases together using hot glue and making sure no two petals are fully touching; this should give you your first earring. Repeat steps for the second earring.

66. Duct Tape Backpack

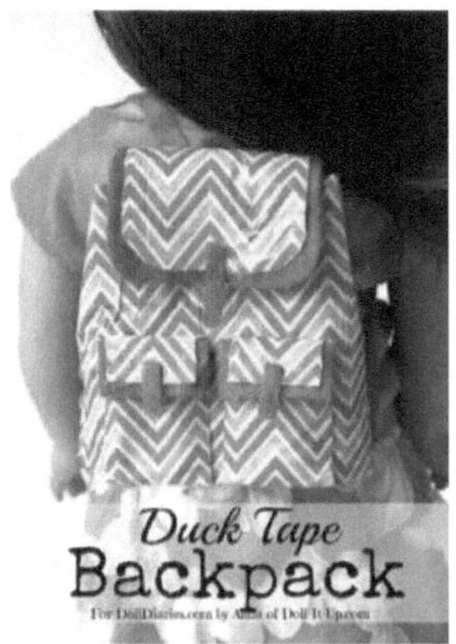

Materials

- Duct tape
- Scissors
- Glue
- Chalk
- Staple gun
- A piece of cardboard, measuring 3 inches by 10½ inches

Directions

1. Make a piece of duct tape solid fabric to measure about 25 inches by 20 inches using any of the many ways shown in this book. Slightly trim all corners of the cardboard to make them slightly rounded. Tape all over the cardboard with duct tape on both sides.

2. Let your fabric stand upright, the shorter side vertical, and fold ½ inch towards the side that you want to be the inside of your backpack. Place the cardboard on the folded section. Be sure that the cardboard touches the walls.

3. Now use the staple gun to staple the cardboard to the folded fabric all the way around the cardboard to make the cardboard the base of your pack. If the fabric is not enough, use more tape to close the gap. If it is more than enough, allow the tape to overlap, and then tape it closed.

4. Slightly pinch two corners on one long side and tape them over to form darts. Carefully tape both inside and outside the base of your backpack so that the staple pins do not show. This will prevent getting scratched, and it will make the bottom stronger.

5. Cut a piece of felt about 10 inches by 7 inches and make the 2 bottom edges slightly rounded. Glue the piece along the top back edge making sure it's smooth. Create a pleat in the middle of the sides of the backpack by pressing the backpack front and back openings together.

6. You want the pockets to be 4 inches by 5 inches. However, you need to cut the rectangles for the pockets to be 12 inches by 6 then fold each of these in half to have 6 inches by 6. Fold in an inch each on three of the sides, and then fold out half an inch of the folded section.

7. Place the pockets in position and paste the half-inch onto the bag using an inch-thick tape. The bottom section requires a little creativity because the folds interfere with each other where they meet. Repeat step using 8-inch by 3½-inch strips to come up with 4 inches by 3½-inch rectangles for the flaps. Tape them just above the pockets, facing up, so that they bend down when closing.

8. Glue a piece of felt to what will be the bottom side of each flap. A small felt border should be left on the three sides. Make a loop and straps for your backpack by gluing together duct tape on one side to felt to match the pockets. The flap can be 2/3 inch by 3 inches but make the straps to suit the length you prefer.

9. Tape the loop to the center top of the backpack, and then tape
   the strap at a slight angle overlapping the loop. Cut a strip of
   felt to lay over this part, putting the straps and loop between
   the backpack and this felt. Tape the bottom of the straps to
   the bottom of the backpack first with hot glue and then with a
   strip of duct tape. Circle the bag twice to secure the straps
   strongly.

67. Water Bottle Holder

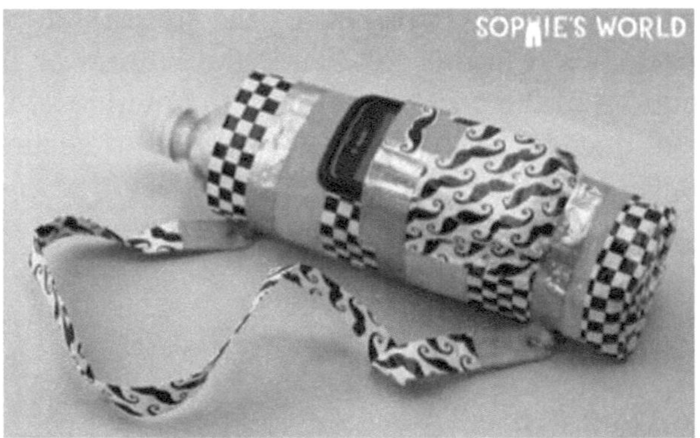

Materials

- Water bottle
- Duct tape
- Scissors
- Tarp
- Two dog clips

Directions

1. Cut a piece of tarp the size of your bottle by holding the tarp against the bottle and rolling it around until there is an inch or two overlapping.

2. Cut the tarp and leave an inch overhanging at the top. Cover the tarp in duct tape making sure all spaces are covered by allowing each piece of tape to slightly overlap the last piece.

3. Clip off all the edges as well as the inside of the tarp and tape. Fold it over any overhanging. Wrap the fabric around your bottle. Seal the seam using a strip of duct tape of the same color, and fold any extra tape over at the ends.

4. Pinch 2 sides of the bottom to form triangles and tape these over thoroughly to form a strong base. Take the bottle out of the tarp mold.

5. Cut 4 inches of tape and place 1 inch inside the top of the fabric at the joint. Fold this strip onto itself and tape the last inch against the outside of the fabric. Repeat on the opposite side.

6. Put the bottle back in, and wrap a strip of tape around the tabs, using the bottle for support. Make the handle the length you desire, fold it over on the vertical side, and then punch holes near the ends on both sides.

7. Punch holes on the tabs of the holder and use dog clips to clip the handle to the tabs.

8. Make a small piece of fabric, just an inch wider than your phone and an inch longer. Place it on the holder and secure it using more strips of duct tape. Make sure to leave it open on top.

Conclusion

Thank you for downloading this book.

I hope that you have enjoyed learning more about duct tape crafts and have been inspired to complete your own projects.

I know that in our house we are never without at least one roll of duct tape. But it is not normally used for home maintenance anymore, and it is more likely to be found in my craft room than in the garage!

With the wide range of duct tapes available, I find that there is no end to the creative projects that I can create. I hope that this book has spurred your own creativity as well.

Whether you are looking for a simple way to liven up a gift or want to challenge yourself to something a little more difficult, you are bound to find a duct tape craft that is suitable for you.

If you have any thoughts on this book, I would really appreciate hearing them. If you have a moment, please review this book on Amazon for me.

Thanks!

Last Chance to Get YOUR Bonus!

FOR A LIMITED TIME ONLY – Get my best-selling book "DIY Crafts: The 100 Most Popular Crafts & Projects That Make Your Life Easier" absolutely FREE!

Readers who have downloaded the bonus book as well have seen the greatest changes in their crafting abilities and have expanded their repertoire of crafts – so it is *highly recommended* to get this bonus book today!

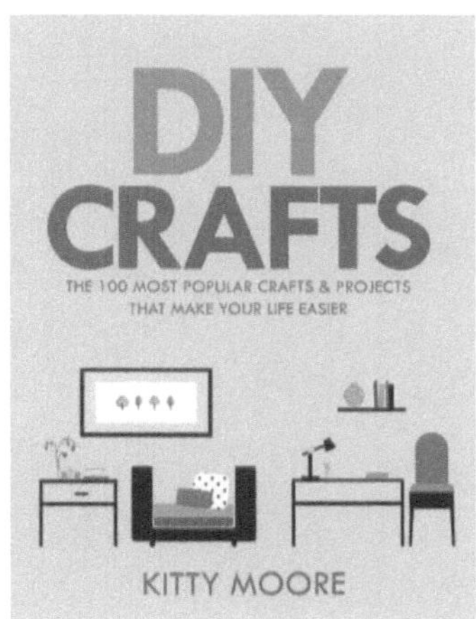

Get your free copy at:

ArtsCraftsAndMore.com/Bonus

Final Words

Thank you for downloading this book!

I really hope that you have been inspired to create your own projects and that you will have a lot of fun crafting.

I do hope that you and your family have found lots of ways to fill lazy afternoons or rainy days in a more fun way.

If you have enjoyed this book and would like to share your positive thoughts, could you please take 30 seconds of your time to go back and give me a review on my Amazon book page!

I really appreciate these reviews because I like to know what people have thought about the book.

Again, thank you and have fun crafting!

Disclaimer

No Warranties: The authors and publishers don't guarantee or warrant the quality, accuracy, completeness, timeliness, appropriateness or suitability of the information in this book, or of any product or services referenced by this site.

The information in this site is provided on an "as is" basis and the authors and publishers make no representations or warranties of any kind with respect to this information. This site may contain inaccuracies, typographical errors, or other errors.

Liability Disclaimer: The publishers, authors, and other parties involved in the creation, production, provision of information, or delivery of this site specifically disclaim any responsibility, and shall not be held liable for any damages, claims, injuries, losses, liabilities, costs, or obligations including any direct, indirect, special, incidental, or consequences damages (collectively known as "Damages") whatsoever and howsoever caused, arising out of, or in connection with the use or misuse of the site and the information contained within it, whether such Damages arise in contract, tort, negligence, equity, statute law, or by way of other legal theory.